Soul Transformation
through Advent

daily devotions from Advent through Epiphany

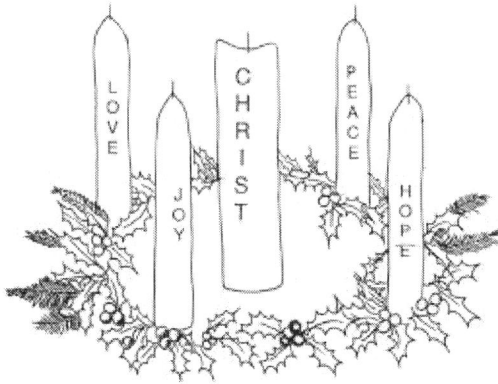

Soul Transformation Through Advent-daily devotions from
Advent through Epiphany
©Copyright Deborah R. Newman 2017
Used by permission from:
www.teatimeforyoursoul.com
All rights reserved.

Dedication

To Lila Ruth Farrow
My Unexpected Gift from Advent 2016

Contents

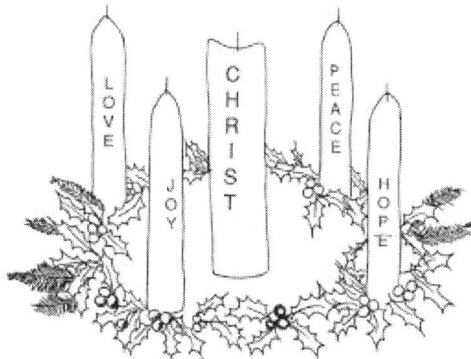

Introduction
Welcome to Advent for your soul....

Christmas can easily become a strange brew of warm memories steeped in a whirlwind of all consuming chores and expectations that can weaken the flavor one would expect from the happiest time of the year. As the season of Advent rolls around again, do you have an unconscious agenda that includes: making sure that absolutely no one is disappointed, creating magical memories, cooking fabulous food that should be eaten without gaining a pound? Does Christmas seem about thinking up and buying perfect presents for everyone you know, sending standout Christmas cards, decorating your home, hosting parties, all completed by December 24th? Do all these tasks drain your soul?

Is the idea of Advent, counting down to Christmas; more of a timer that you race against to prove your worth than a holy wonder because of the birth of Christ? If so, you are not alone. If it weren't for the annual Silent Retreat the weekend before Thanksgiving in 2000 I don't know if I could have ever found the strength to let go of my own self-destructive expectations regarding Christmas. Christmas pressure began infecting my soul in the way a bad winter virus can spoil even a perfect Christmas season. When I stopped long enough to let the Holy Spirit reveal my unconscious thinking I wrote this thought—"I hate Christmas!" I went on to consider why. I journaled how the dread of the tasks required of me when I arrived back home had become an impossible feat. My Christmas lament flooded the page like a rusted-out water heater bursting its sides. I ended my diatribe with this thought. "I wonder what it would be like to come back as a man at Christmas." Now, I can laugh that it was the best I could come up with in my carnal state of mind, though at the time I was totally serious.

I had no idea that my innocent turn of the century musing had actually been the crack the Holy Spirit used to open my heart to soul transformation at Advent. I honestly had no intention of doing anything different that year, or any year after that. However, the Holy Spirit is always working things together for my good, and year after year, I made subtle changes that led me to open true gift of Advent.

A few years before that silent retreat, I began using Advent devotions, an advent wreath and candles, to guide my children's minds away from the obsessive focus on Santa and teach them about the true meaning of Christmas. It worked for them. They loved reading the child-sized devotions. They participated by lighting and blowing out candles, as they developed the expertise to do so. The Advent devotions created special memories to them and me. I began writing Tea Time for Your Soul Devotions (my weekly email devotional thought) on the subject of Advent each season. I began purposeful and meaningful changes around the season of Christmas and what I expected of it. It wasn't Santa Claus that was stealing my Christmas, rather it was the expectations I put on myself. I discovered that I needed Advent even more than my children in order to experience the real joy of the season.

I love spending Christmas in traditional ways. I love to bake sugar cookies with a twist of lemon rind. My white chocolate popcorn, that delights everyone, is so simple to make and brings back happy memories.* Christmas is a most wonderful time of the year and I look forward to concerts, movies and travel. What I refuse to miss; what I won't live without is the realization that the Church Fathers' so wisely prescribed through the season of Advent—a transformation for your soul. Before there were Christmas gifts, Santa Claus or even Christmas trees, there was Advent. Advent is a path to new beginnings. In fact, Advent marks the beginning of the church calendar. It signals a fresh start spiritually.

The focus on Advent as a season of soul transformation really serves me now as I am often in the position of spending Christmas in nontraditional ways. Sometimes I cannot be with family. I have even been in a non-Christian country during Christmas. Because my Advent focus I can have a full experience of Christmas no matter my circumstances, because Advent happens in my soul! I have found the thing that cannot be taken away from me no matter what my Christmas season holds.

In Advent, I anticipate the truths of Christmas showing me what is truest about me, whom I am and why I am here. My soul opens to a reality that transcends the traditional warmth from the season. When I really listen to the message of Christmas and receive God's gift of His Son (not what a Hallmark Christmas commercial displays); I am transformed. Each week of December, I count down to Christmas through the time-honored tradition of lighting a candle for Advent. I invite you to come along with me. I hope you will find guidance for getting off the Christmas Pleasing Merry-Go-Round and come upon the true hope, love, joy and peace that Christmas brings.

The children's devotion we used in our home ordered the four candles of advent as hope—the prophets' candle, love-the Bethlehem candle, joy—the Shepherd candle and peace—the Angel candle. There are many variations and there is no exact order to the four weeks of Advent. But what I have found is that almost all advent devotions make Hope the first candle we light.

I like to light the candles of Advent in my home even now when I don't have children living with me. You don't need to have a wreath to focus your soul on advent. If you wish, you can use an Advent Wreath as a decoration and a reminder of the season. You can make your own wreath gathering four candles and some evergreen. There are many commercial products available as well.

Here are some ideas about the spiritual significance of the Advent Wreath. These are not absolutes but may give some inspiration about how and why an Advent Wreath became a part of the season.

Significance of the Advent Wreath
Evergreen wreath—green for the spiritual growth
Light of candles—Light of Christ
3 Purple Candles—preparation through repentance
1 Pink Candle—lit the third Sunday of Advent—signals anticipation and the brightening as the light of Christ gets closer, or transition from repentance to anticipation of Christ's return
White Christ Candle in the middle of wreath—lit only on Christmas day signifies the first and second coming of Christ to this earth.

My daughter was in preschool and my son a toddler when we began our simple Sunday Advent Devotions. The children loved to blow out the candles and as they were able they began to light candles, read the scripture or even lead the family devotion time. I have included a page with a very simple family devotion each week of Advent similar to what we shared in our home. My children added their personal touches to our Advent worship time. My daughter learned a song in Kindergarten that she led us in singing: "Light one candle for (hope, love, joy, peace—different word each week); One bright candle for hope, He brings hope to every heart, He comes. He comes." My son brought home a ceramic candle holder he made in school specifically for the Christ candle. I still use it every year. He painted it with an array of colors that remind us of the life of Christ. I've suggested carols that you can find on the internet and sing or play from your device. I also give a simple Scripture reading of the Christmas story and a verse from Romans that highlights each virtue of Advent that coordinates with the week. I have one simple question to ask around the table. I hope celebrating Advent will bring your family the special memories it brought my family.

Christmas Season begins on Christmas Day. In the west, liturgical churches acknowledge a twelve-day festival, starting on December 25 and ending on January 5. It is known as Christmastide, Christmas Season, or the twelve days of Christmas. This is the season between the Feast of the Nativity (Christmas Day) and the Feast of Epiphany (January 6---celebrating the visit of the Magi). Though Advent ends with Christmas Day, this devotion will focus on the 12 Days of Christmas. It will guide you to consider the experiences you have lived this past Christmas and Holiday season and help you digest the lessons you have learned. The Feast of Nativity (Christmas Day) and the Feast of the Epiphany are immoveable feasts, meaning they have fixed dates of December 25 and January 6 respectively. Advent is a movable holiday. The first Sunday of Advent will vary according to the day of the week December 25 falls in the calendar in a particular year. My granddaughter was born on November on the first Sunday of Advent, but her birthday will not always be during the season of Advent. Advent begins on the fourth Sunday before Christmas and occasionally that makes the first Sunday of Advent in November.

During the twelve days of Christmas, the calendar will change. You will have a whole new year ahead of you. It's a perfect time to spend extra focus on your soul and ways you can live each day of the new year with purpose and meaning. I like to keep my Christmas tree and lights up until Epiphany. This way I get to enjoy them after the hustle of Christmas is over.

Spiritual Disciplines for Advent.

1. Be kind to yourself. Most holiday stress comes from thinking you have to please everybody. Do less this year. Say "No" to some things with confidence. Know that saying "yes" to every person, party invitation, and charity will definitely land you in the stressed-out zone. Realize that the world can go on without you, but you cannot go on without proper sleep, exercise and mental relaxation.
2. Be joyful. Hum along to Christmas tunes. Make it the most wonderful time of the year, because it is. Jesus came to earth to make it possible for you to have a relationship with God. That is something to celebrate. Practice praying without ceasing by asking God to show you the joy in each task: wrapping gifts, decorating, baking, card writing, shopping, and all the others.
3. Be a loving presence by enjoying the joyful people and prepare for grumpy ones. Make sure you have time to share joyful moments with others this year. And for those negative people who live in your house, or you will visit this holiday season; accept their faults. Don't let yourself be abused by them, but don't let unforgiveness extinguish your holiday cheer.

Welcome to a Soul Transforming Advent!

*I've included the recipes I mentioned on page 56.

First Sunday of Advent-Light One Candle for Hope
Prophet's Candle

1. Light one purple candle: for Hope
2. Sing: "I Heard the Bells on Christmas Day" or "O Little Town of Bethlehem"
3. Read: Luke 1:67-80 and Romans 5:5
4. Share: What are you hoping for this Christmas?

First Sunday of Advent
Waiting with Hope

On the first day of Advent 2016, I awoke to a call at 3:20 am that I should come to the hospital because my daughter was being taken down to deliver Lila—my first grandchild! I had been alerted to her early arrival two days before when Rachel's water broke, but not much labor. I arrived in Birmingham, Alabama from Dallas, Texas seven and a half hours later (it would have been sooner but there wasn't a direct flight!). And then...we waited. We waited on Lila's lungs to respond to a couple of steroid shots (she was three weeks early). As we waited, we halfway watched football and occasionally made small talk about subjects other than Lila's birth; but mainly we carried on just wishing, wondering and thinking we could plan for the time that Lila would arrive based on the medical advice we were given. All we could think about was what we were waiting for, our baby girl to come into the world.

While waiting on Lila, a code blue was called to her room; then the number was changed to the room next door. We Grandparents huddled and prayed for the baby hoping it wasn't ours but doing the only thing we could do while we waited. Now we were waiting and shedding a few tears and offering more intense prayers. The waiting got rocky at this point. My devotional thought for the day was: *received a faith as precious as ours* (2 Peter 1:1). In those moments of not knowing if our 3-week-early baby, whose mother's water had broken 40 hours earlier, was in trouble, I had a faith as precious as ours. My sister-in-law texted me that she was praying; she didn't need to know the inner struggle at this point, but I was so grateful for that text that confirmed a precious faith. As time went on with no news, we were able to confirm that our baby was just taking a few hours to push out into the world so we waited with deeper relief. I decided to write my Tea Time for Your Soul for Advent while I waited.

I was literally writing this devotion when my son-in-law walked out, tears flowing down, to bear the great news of her healthy birth and healthy mom and beautiful baby. The wait was over. It wasn't four Sundays of Advent, rather a 40-hour labor and delivery, but it was filled with all the ups and downs and mundane moments of life.

This most recent experience of intense waiting challenges me and reminds me that waiting is what my life with God is all about. I'm challenged because I have never had the experience of not being able to get His return for me off my mind as I did waiting on my first granddaughter. I'm reminded that waiting is what life is about. I'm grateful that God was with me, steadying me in the wait as He does every day that I wait for His return. I want to learn to wait in the same way Paul did, thinking about it every day as he revealed to Timothy and all of us in 2 Timothy 4:8: "*Now there is in store for me the crown of righteousness, which the Lord, the righteous Judge, will award to me on that day—and not only to me, but also to all who have longed for his appearing.*"

Advent re-orientates our souls to what our lifetimes are all about—waiting. The gift of Advent is an annual practice of waiting with hope.

First Monday of Advent
Immanuel—God With Us

Announcing the arrival of my first grandchild in the world was the most joyful news I could share. We knew her name. We knew she was coming. Yet, when she was finally here with us, everything changed. Wanting her, knowing she existed, and actually being able to hold her in our arms and look into her little eyes are two different realities.

Advent draws our thoughts towards the beyond-joyful news that God shared over 2000 years ago. God's news spread throughout the whole world and continues to encircle the globe. This news was broadcasted long before our modern media communication tools. After the angels startled the shepherds by announcing the birth of Jesus, the people of God have taken it from there. The church can't stop sharing the reality of what it means that our Lord and Savior Jesus Christ came to our world to be one of us. He did this so that God could restore any who will put faith in Jesus Christ to become one with Him.

As we prepare to gather in crowded churches on Christmas Eve, let us consider how we have become proclaimers of this good news. How do we experience God with us, and how does that impact the news we discuss? Do we digest the police shootings, riots, protests, unrest in this world in light of the Good News?

God is with me. He entered this fallen world. He told me that a day is coming when He will make all things new. Just as He kept His promise to send the Messiah through a virgin in the town of Bethlehem, He will keep His promise to return a second time as King. In the in-between, He wants me to spread the Good News.

We celebrate the unimaginable promise God fulfilled in the unexpected way—He, God, became one of us so that we can become one with Him. The way that I become one with Him is through repentance and recognition of my utter inability to be holy. God tells me that my faith in His Son's righteousness creates a seed of holiness in me which creates the potential for oneness with God. When Christ comes again, my holiness will become a true reality, but in between He gives me the power to experience tastes of holiness through the Holy Spirit who lives in me.

God sent Jesus, Immanuel, to be one with us just as the prophets foretold. God sends all who become one with Jesus to share His great salvation. He longs for the whole world to become one with Him. As Peter explains: *The Lord is not slow in keeping his promise, as some understand slowness. Instead he is patient with you, not wanting anyone to perish, but everyone to come to repentance* (2 Peter 3:9). He also instructs how we can best broadcast the Good News until the day He comes to earth the second time: *Live such good lives among the pagans that, though they accuse you of doing wrong, they may see your good deeds and glorify God on the day he visits us.* (1 Peter 2:12).

How does your life share the too-good-to-be-true-good-news of Immanuel—God with us?

First Tuesday in Advent
Make it a Holy Season

Advent is not the first time I have been reminded that Christmas is coming. Christmas decorations have been rolling out in all the stores since before Halloween. It is the first time I accept Christmas. It is the week I begin turning my heart to what the season is meant to be all about. As I begin to experience Christmas again this year, I need to hold my heart open to the holiness of the season or I have no chance of making it a holy season.

It starts with fighting off the world and all its trappings at Christmas. There is nothing holy about frantically buying gifts I can't afford, packing my schedule with events and parties that drain my energy, and eating every delight that is set before me.

The season begins with high hopes that will be fulfilled only if I set my hope on Jesus. He brings hope to every heart! Hope will help us make this season a holy season. One of the reasons that I set out an Advent wreath on my kitchen table is to help me maintain my focus on the holiness of this time of year. The circle of evergreen dotted by a candle to light each week with the white candle in the middle, reminds me of Christ, untainted by the other trappings of Christmas. It invites me to remember that Christmas is holy.

You have to orientate your soul to feel hope because hope is about what is not seen. Christmas is thrown in your face and can distract you from hope. The first candle of Christmas is called the Prophet's candle. The prophets held on to the hope that God would do what He said He would do. Year after year they held on to the promise of the Messiah even though hundreds of years passed without a sign of Him.

Holiness was everywhere Jesus was while He lived on this earth. Not everyone recognized His holy presence. There is holiness in the air at Christmas, but it can easily be overcome by all the pressure and pleasures the season offers.

I will live in holy hope as I focus on my living King. He is in heaven reigning over the spiritual kingdom that will never leave me hopeless. I have more reason than the Israelites in Isaiah's day to believe in the light that has come. Isaiah 9 talks about the child that is born with a special introduction in verse 2, "*The people walking darkness have seen a great light; on those living in the land of the shadow of death a light has dawned.*"

The first two weeks of Advent are meant to focus on holiness through repentance. When we ponder the need for Christ to empty Himself and take on human flesh we are confronted with the reason for His drastic, sacrificial action is that it was the only way for sinners to be redeemed. Take some time this first week of Advent to ask God to search your heart and reveal the sin that Christ came to earth to conquer in your soul.

First Wednesday in Advent
Joseph, a man of great hope

God plans every detail of our lives. He offers us the opportunity to join Him in His work. He prepared good works for every one of us to do for His glory (Ephesians 2:10). God had big plans for Joseph's life. No one would have suspected that Joseph, the gentle carpenter, would become the step-father to God.

Fathers always play a back-stage role when their wives are having a baby. Joseph was no exception. What we know of Joseph from Scripture is very limited. We do know that he was a loving follower of God. We know that God gave him a special responsibility while he lived on this earth and, from all indications; it seems that he fulfilled his role very well. Even when Joseph first heard that Mary was pregnant, he didn't respond in wounded jealousy. He knew that he shouldn't marry a woman who had been unfaithful to him, but he didn't want to publicly disgrace her. He was not a hothead either. He could have reacted right away; we know he at least took one night to sleep on it because the Scripture tells us that God spoke to him in a dream (Matthew 1:18-25).

God's message to Joseph changed his view of his options. The angel told him that he should take Mary as his wife because she was pregnant by the Holy Spirit. Joseph did everything the angel told him to do. He married Mary, kept her a virgin and named the baby Jesus. He went beyond that to providing for his Son, teaching Him the craft of carpentry, and providing religious training. The last time we know of Joseph was when Jesus was 12 and was left in Jerusalem. Joseph was by Mary's side as they searched the city for their budding teenage son. When they found Jesus, it was Mary who spoke. Joseph was in the background. We think that Joseph probably died before Jesus' public ministry. We know he was not living when Jesus hung on the cross because one of Jesus' seven sayings from the cross was putting His mother into the care of John the Apostle since she was a widow.

As we enter the Christmas season this year and reflect on Joseph, he is a great example of how to live your life as a pleasing sacrifice to God (Romans 12:1-2). Joseph didn't have to be in the spotlight to serve God. He was willing to be in the background. It's important to remember that service in the background does not go unnoticed by God. Most of us are like Joseph, the good works that God has prepared for us to do won't get much attention from the world. Maybe God created you to share the gospel with your neighbor. Perhaps there is something about your personality or your story that will reach a person as no one else could. Maybe God's good works for you are to volunteer at a homeless shelter, perhaps in the back room sorting the clothes, the job everyone hates to do. Good works come in all sizes, big and small. Each good work is as important to God as the other. Why not take a lesson from Joseph and live your life accepting the good works God asks of you. I'm sure it will help you have a Merry Christmas.

First Thursday in Advent
The Innkeeper at Bethlehem Providing Hope for Shelter

Every Christmas pageant must have an innkeeper. His part in the Christmas story appears at a critical moment. The suspense turns tragic as the famous innkeeper turns the pregnant couple away. At last he redeems himself somewhat by offering the shelter of his barn. Any child is proud to play the role of the Innkeeper in the annual Christmas pageant.

Interesting, it is not a role that is written in the real Christmas story contained in the Gospels. The only mention of the inn is the context of an explanation for why Mary and Joseph placed Jesus in a manger. The Innkeeper has become popular from the dramatic retelling of the story, not from the Gospels.

How did Mary and Joseph end up outside of an inn and where the animals are kept? There were inns in the time that Jesus was born, but they were usually in larger cities. Jesus Himself referred to an Innkeeper in the parable He told about the Good Samaritan. It is probable that no inn existed in the town of Bethlehem because it was such a small village. The term inn can be interpreted "a place of lodging," thus it did not necessarily indicate a hotel type residence. In fact, an inn could be used to describe the way a caravan of people made lodging together as they traveled. Their animals and belongings would be right beside them as they settled up for the night, usually around a public well for safety and convenience.

What kind of inn was it that offered no room for Mary and Joseph? It might have been that Mary and Joseph came to the home of one of their relatives, along with all the other relations who were required to travel to Bethlehem to register for the census. Perhaps they were offered hospitality and food, but when it came to finding a private place to have a baby, their needs were unique from the others who had sought shelter. Perhaps they were sent out to the place the animals were kept in order to find the privacy they needed for the birth of their child. The manger, the feeding trough for the animals, was a creative makeshift cradle for the time they spent sleeping outside.

We must not conceive of the Innkeeper as an inhospitable, barely compassionate brute. Perhaps we can look at him as a loving family member, offering the best of convenience to his special relatives who had traveled a long distance. The fact that there was no room in the inn was not an indication that Jesus wasn't welcomed and wanted by the people in Bethlehem. Indeed, preparations were made for His birth; even though they didn't think of Him as their Savior, they thought of Him as their relative and they wanted to create the best environment possible for His birth.

It makes me think about the readiness of my own heart. Have I made every preparation possible to welcome Jesus into the home of my heart? Will I make whatever adjustments are necessary in order to give Him the best place possible in my thoughts, hopes, and dreams this Christmas? It seems Jesus' relatives at the inn where Joseph and Mary sought refuge made room for Jesus. What about you?

16

First Friday in Advent
Hoping to display Virtue

How have you been feeling so far this Advent season? Have you had regular times of stillness and wonder about God and what He did by sending His Son to earth as a baby? Are you smiling more this season? Are you getting more rest or less?

I can relate to you if you have to admit that you find yourself losing ground rather than making spiritual progress during the Advent season. Do you ever wonder why? After all your attempts to make this Christmas different from last year you still yell at your family members, you spend too much money, you over-commit to parties. It's not just you. You have a cunning adversary who is constantly looking to trip you up. Satan tempts us when we are weak. I know that I can grow spiritually weak during the Advent season. If I don't watch out.

Jesus was weak when Satan tempted Him. Satan waited until Jesus was the most tired and hungry before he set in after Him out in the wilderness. Be aware, your adversary the devil, is constantly looking for ways to trip you up. Don't you just know that he is behind the crazy mess that Christmas has become for so many? We are told in 1 Peter 5:8 to be alert to the devil. Be alert that he wants to steal the love, joy and peace of Christmas. The best way you can keep Satan from stealing your Christmas is to take some time to sit still and take in what Advent has to teach us.

We not only need to be alert to Satan and find time for stillness, but we also need to heed Jesus' example in how to resist him. Jesus used God's Words from the Bible to fight off the temptations Satan brought before Him. God's Word is the best possible way to fight off temptation.

Here are some words to help you fight Satan during Advent. When you catch that nasty spirit Christmas brings out in the post office line the mad dash for the most in-demand toy quote Psalm 37:7:

"Be still before the Lord and wait patiently for him; do not fret when men succeed in their ways, when they carry out their wicked schemes."

When you get overwhelmed by the parties, baking and things you need to do, remember Isaiah 40:30-33:

"Even youths grow tired and weary, and young men stumble and fall; but those who hope in the Lord will renew their strength. They will soar on wings like eagle; they will run and not grow weary, they will walk and not be faint."

When you find yourself being angry with the people in your household, remember that your precious Heavenly Father is slow to anger and He can help you be that way too:

"And he passed in front of Moses, proclaiming, The LORD, the LORD, the compassionate and gracious God, slow to anger, abounding in love and faithfulness." (Exodus 34:6).

Remember, it's not the Grinch who stole Christmas, but you do have an enemy who wants to keep you from fully receiving the message of God's love this Advent Season.

17

First Saturday in Advent
How NOT to Have a Merry Christmas

Have you been listening to the Christmas advertisements? I challenge you to stop and fully receive the message of Christmas they bring. They tell you that the true joy of the season is found by purchasing their latest bargain for someone you love, but they don't stop there. The real enticement is to get you to think more about yourself. The messages end by encouraging you to buy gifts on sale for your friends and family and save most of your money picking up something you really want. After all, the advertisements imply, you are sure to get bad gifts.

When I think of the messages I receive about Christmas from the world, it sends me running back to Christ to find the true meaning of Christmas. Jesus didn't come as a baby so that I could have a rationale for splurging on myself once a year. He didn't come to wear me out chasing a dream holiday. He didn't come so that I would remember the homeless and hungry only in December. He came to be my Savior. He came to make a relationship with God possible.

He also put me in charge of telling others about the true meaning of Christmas. It's sad to think about how empty Christmas is without Jesus, yet that is exactly what Christmas is like for over half the people you live, work and interact with each year. They are living the dream of Christmas that will never satisfy. Even if they could buy everything they wanted for themselves and everyone they love, they would never be satisfied.

When I listen to the messages from the world around Christmas, I sense the empty feelings so many must be experiencing as another Christmas comes and goes through their lives. They were created for a personal relationship with Jesus Christ, not to replace their disappointment with Aunt Gertrude's sweater with a shiny new car. And by the way, what is so wrong with wearing Aunt Gertrude's crazy Christmas sweater with a smile and wrapping yourself in the warm feelings that, though she doesn't have the best taste in clothes, she does love her niece enough to buy that gift?

If you want to miss out on a Merry Christmas, listen to the advertisements that bombard you every day. If you want to have a Merry Christmas, reflect on the life of the baby that was born. He lived His life focused on loving His Heavenly Father and telling everyone how much He loved them. I just read an article this week about what the unchurched think of Christians and most of them said that they would attend church with us if we will ask. The best way to have a Merry Christmas is to share the story of Christmas with those who don't know, but who have hearts that were designed to accept the story.

This year I hope you will spread the joy of Christmas to the people in your world who do not know Jesus. Take some time to pray and ask God to show you someone with whom you can share His love at Christmas this year.

Second Sunday of Advent-Light One Candle for Love
Bethlehem Candle

Light two purple candles: for Hope and Love
Sing: "Love Came Down at Christmas" or "O Come All Ye Faithful"
Read: Matthew 1:18-25 and Romans 5:8
Share: When have you felt loved at Christmas? How can you share love at Christmas?

Second Sunday in Advent
Love Involves Waiting Without

On the second Sunday of Advent, in which my granddaughter Lila was born, I had to leave my post as chief-cook-and-bottle-washer. It's a role every grandmother covets and carries out with the greatest of love. Since I lived several states away, I wouldn't be able to see her again for three weeks. Perhaps this absence of what we most want is part of the reason we distract ourselves from the spiritual gift of Advent. Maybe it is the angst of waiting that compelled us to create fantasies of gifts, parties, feasts, and endless shopping during the season of Advent. It's hard to feel the absence of what you most desire when your mind is totally preoccupied otherwise.

When John the Baptist began preaching and baptizing in the wilderness, he was in the same state as we find ourselves at Advent. The Messiah's coming had been prophesied hundreds of years before. and the state of Israel was desperately in need of rescue from the oppressive Roman government. It was a time much like our own. John, however, insisted that those who wanted to be ready to meet Jesus should focus on preparing and making their paths straight. He said:

> "*In those days John the Baptist came, preaching in the wilderness of Judea and saying, Repent, for the kingdom of heaven has come near. This is he who was spoken of through the prophet Isaiah: A voice of one calling in the wilderness, Prepare the way for the Lord, make straight paths for him*" (Matthew 3:1-2).

Clearly there are fulfilling spiritual tasks to focus on in Advent. Advent is not just about twiddling your thumbs, waiting on what you really want. Advent calls you to active waiting. You will not miss Advent if you prepare and make your paths straight. Traditionally these four weeks before Christmas were days of fasting up until the Christmas Feast when they celebrated Christ's birth with great joy prepared for by a hungry tummy. It's an extremely difficult season to fast these days in our culture. In fact, you probably need to eat a high protein diet to keep up with the physically demanding tasks such as putting up Christmas lights, increasing your social life by attending parties and all that shopping!

However, you can prepare and make your paths straight by creating a quiet space just between you and your Lord each day of Advent. When you think about Christ's advent to the earth you think about love. Christ left heaven to enter this earth as a helpless, tiny babe. How much love filled His heart for Him to come to earth, knowing He would be rejected and crucified? He came because of His great love for us, not wishing that any would live in a fallen world forever. Have there been some loveless moments during your Advent wait so far? Maybe you got in a fight with your spouse about how much money you spent. Maybe you grumbled loud enough for others to hear when someone jumped in line ahead of those who were waiting longer.

What is it that you most want but do not have?

Second Monday in Advent
Loved and Favored

In this season of Advent Season I am reminded of God's great favor toward mankind. Even though the church fathers designated the four Sundays before Christmas as the beginning of the church year and a season of penitence and self-examination; it didn't take long for the season of Advent to become a season of joy, anticipation and celebration.

I can easily understand why. It is hard to meditate on the Christmas story without becoming simply overwhelmed by God's favor. His favor towards us and great love for us overwhelms the reality of our sin.

Isn't that why God sent Jesus? Often there are negative realities that come with the season of Advent. The absence of a loved one, busyness, pressure from Christmas tasks, and debt are a few examples. Yet, everyone can feel favored if they will let their hearts open to the messages of Advent.

Mary, the peasant girl chosen one to be the mother of our Savior, was favored. The angel Gabriel told her, *"Greetings, you who are highly favored! The Lord is with you."* (Luke 1:28). She wasn't the only one. When the angels came to the shepherds the night of Jesus birth, they announced, *"Glory to God in the highest, and on earth peace to men on whom his favor rests"*(Luke 2:14).

I love the truth that we are all favored by God. In our human relationships, we are always seeking to be the favorite. We want to be the favorite child, the favorite boss, the favorite employee. We think that others have to be out of favor in order for us to be the favorite. The reality with God's favor is that I can experience myself as deeply favored by God and not take away from any of the favor He has for you. He has enough favor to go around to all of us.

Perhaps the greatest way that God showed His utter favor for mankind in all of human history was by sending Jesus. Though His heart ached from Jesus' absence along with the anticipated torture and His coming death for the sins of all, God's favor for mankind outweighed His personal loss and suffering.

Advent is a season of anticipation and patience—looking for Jesus' second coming. It is also a season to celebrate the sense of being highly favored by the God of the Universe.

It almost wants to make me break out in song and rejoicing. Though I am a sinner, God has bestowed great favor on me. I want to sing like Mary, *"My soul glorifies the Lord and my spirit rejoices in God my Savior, for he has been mindful of the humble state of his servant. From now on all generations will call me blessed."* (Luke 1:46-48).

Are you mindful of your favored state?

Do you call yourself blessed?

How does confessing your sins reveal God's favor at Advent?

Second Tuesday in Advent
Love Reveals Divine Absurdities

There are so many Divine Absurdities in this life. God just does not see this world the way we do. We tend to look to our bank accounts, the sizes of our houses, the trips we can take, to measure our blessings. It's not that way with God.

It was at the moment of incarnation that Mary, the mother of Jesus, understood the reality of Divine Absurdities most fully in her own life. When Jesus came into her life, she understood the deep realities of this world that so many miss. She had better insight into God than the greatest theologians who ever lived. Read what she says about God;

And Mary said: My soul glorifies the Lord, and my spirit rejoices in God my Savior, for he has been mindful of the humble state of his servant. From now on all generations will call me blessed, for the Mighty One has done great things for me—holy is his name. His mercy extends to those who fear him, from generation to generation. He has performed mighty deeds with his arm; he has scattered those who are proud in their inmost thoughts. He has brought down rulers from their thrones but has lifted up the humble. He has filled the hungry with good things, but has sent the rich away empty. He has helped his servant Israel, remembering to be merciful to Abraham and his descendants forever, just as he promised our ancestors. (Luke 1:46-55)

One of the Divine Absurdities that stands out to me in this song from Mary's heart is that He has filled the hungry with good things, but has sent the rich away empty. I never feel this more intensely than when I am in the presence of the world's poor. The poor are literally hungry. What they wouldn't do if they were able to eat the scraps that I throw away after dinner. I recognize my own extravagance when I am in a third world country and take my daily supplements. Even though I always get a decent amount of food each day, I also add some vitamins and minerals that I think my body needs. Yet, these hungry people are filled with good things, while the rich go away empty.

The sad thing is that the rich don't even know they are empty. They are so full of their riches that they don't realize how empty they are. I couldn't recognize my emptiness in my richness either. I can't see my emptiness until I attend church with the poor. Their love and devotion to God is what shows me how little I really have. I know not all poor are satisfied with good things, and just because you are rich doesn't mean you are empty.

It's important to think about the Divine Absurdities in this life. Forgiveness is one. Loving your enemies is one of the most absurd of all. Living by the truth of these Divine Absurdities will make you break forth in song. Mary was speaking for us all when she said that God has been mindful of the humble state of His servant. The greatest of all God's Divine Absurdities is that Jesus Christ's sinless life can be transferred into us. I really love His Divine plans; perhaps they aren't so absurd after all.

Second Wednesday in Advent
Unwrapped Gift of Love

Who has ever heard of someone not unwrapping their gifts at Christmas? I remember a woman telling me the story of growing up very poor during the depression and drawing the number for the most beautiful gift under the tree in her school classroom gift exchange. She told me how she thought it was so extraordinary that she didn't even unwrap it when the other children were tearing their gifts open. She protected it from the snow on her walk home and put it by her bed so she could continue admiring the splendor of its packaging. She had more joy about the wrapping than the gift.

The whole world has been given a gift to unwrap. It is the greatest, most valuable gift that will ever be given. Its wrapping is multifaceted, with images of a tiny baby surrounded by admiring adults and animals, a crucified Savior, a prayerful teacher, a ruling majesty, a Divine incomprehensible figure to behold. The gift of course is Jesus Christ. God gave Him to the world (John 3:16). Unfortunately, this gift has simply been refused by the majority of the inhabitants of this world. The world loves the wrappings of Christmas rather than the gift of Jesus.

It's more than a shame, really; it breaks the heart of God. God has worked hard to offer this gift; it has been given with the greatest of personal sacrifice. It should be the most precious gift anyone has ever received.

Though God continues to offer the gift of His Son, the majority of the world still rejects His great favor. Jesus' very own hometown rejected the gift of Christmas. Luke 4:14-30 records the Sabbath when Jesus was asked to read the day's Scripture which opened to Isaiah 61:1-2. He read, *The Spirit of the Lord is on me, because he has anointed me to preach good news to the poor. He has sent me to proclaim freedom for the prisoners and recovery of sight for the blind, to release the oppressed, to proclaim the year of the Lord's favor* (Luke 4:18-19). Then He sat down and told them that today this scripture was fulfilled before them (Luke 4:21). And they were at first amazed, then angry enough to drive him out of town.

The people of Nazareth are a microcosm of the world at large. We have been offered this amazing gift. We have been told about the year of the Lord's favor. What we believe about this information will define our eternal destiny. The gift is given for the taking. The offer is free and unlimited. There are no lines in which to wait in or post office boxes in which to pick it up. It is simply the most glorious gift offered by the ultimate Giver. It is simply up to us to receive the gift of the Lord's favor. It is very important to keep in mind that if you refuse the gift of the Lord's favor you will not be able to avoid the day of vengeance of our God (Isaiah 61:2).

I pray that you have received your gift of salvation and that you are discovering how incomparable this gift is to all other gifts you have ever received.

How have you unwrapped God's gift to you again this Christmas?

Second Thursday in Advent
Whom or What Do You Love?

If you are not sure whom or what you love, just check out your checkbook. Look around your house at the way you decorate. You will quickly discern whom or what you love. It is important to ponder the object of your love for the sake of your soul.

Jesus said that all the commandments can be fulfilled by loving God with all your heart, mind and soul and your neighbor as yourself (Matthew 22:37-39). Tina Turner may have asked *What's love got to do with it?* But God says that love has everything to do with it.

The second week of Advent is a strategic time to examine whom or what you love. The focus of your love will determine the health of your soul. There is only one way to have a healthy soul and that is to love God. If you do not love God with all your heart, mind and soul, you will love the world. You cannot have a healthy soul when you love the world. St. Augustine said that we either love God to the point of self-contempt or we love ourselves to the point of contempt for God. Augustine doesn't define self-contempt as a hatred of oneself, rather as a freedom from single minded focus on one's selfish desires and pleasures. I think a better way to say it is that we either love God so much that we are free of our own self-focus, or we love the world so much that we have lost a sense of God.

When you love God to the full extent of your human ability to love you will discover that you so completely trust Him that He could tell you the craziest thing and you will be obedient. That's the kind of love you see in Mary after the angel came to tell her that she was going to be pregnant with the promised Messiah. Mary is a perfect example of the effect loving God has on a soul.

Luke 1:26-38 records this interaction between God's messenger, Gabriel, and the young woman, Mary, the one who would become the mother to our Lord. Surely Mary could not fully understand the complete message the angel brought her that day. Love doesn't have to understand; what love needs is to trust. Mary showed the love we think about at Advent. Mary's words, *May it be to me as you have said* (Luke 1:38) can also be translated, *I love you God.*

When you love God, you think more highly of spiritual realities than physical realities. When you love God, you don't get caught up in the appeal of the world. When you love God, you begin to notice you are not as focused on yourself and your needs.

Love is an incredible emotion. Love can rescue your soul from despair and emptiness. Loving God and loving your neighbor the way you naturally love yourself is the greatest experience this earth has to offer.

Who do you love well?

Who do you have trouble loving?

Second Friday in Advent

The second candle of Advent is the Bethlehem Candle and it symbolizes the preparations made to receive the Christ child born in Bethlehem . It is the candle of Love because making preparations for Christ to be born required a lot of love and sacrifice. Mary had to be prepared by her love and devotion to God to be considered for the calling of being the mother to Jesus. Joseph's heart had to be radically transformed by love for Mary and trust in God, not to divorce her, but to accept that the child was God's Son and that his fiancé was still a virgin. It was love for Mary that motivated Joseph to be so persistent in finding the shelter of a stable in a town without vacancies. The couple lovingly received their son and tenderly cared for Him by wrapping Him in warm cloths and making a bed for him from the manger. Love and preparations are rarely noticed. It is usually the final product that gets all the attention. Lighting a candle for love is putting the emphasis on the way you prepare for Christmas, as much as what happens on that day.

Just like Mary and Joseph there is a lot you must do to prepare for Christmas this year. You might be packing for a journey, or preparing for the birth of a baby as I was in the Advent of 2016. Most of us are preparing by shopping, baking, decorating. All of the things we do for Christmas require preparation. The preparing and the planning are not necessarily easy. Everyone loves the final result, but most underestimate the work and effort involved. It takes sacrifice, work and planning to make Christmas come together..

When you light a candle for love this advent, let it remind you to keep love in your heart through all your preparations. That means when you sit with your blinker on prepared to pull into a parking space and someone comes in from the right and steals it from you; you can choose love for God and drive on, rather than cussing and screaming. If the perfect gift you were so excited about buying doesn't even get a word of thanks, move on without withholding acceptance.

Many don't realize that giving real love at Christmas involves delegating responsibilities to others. Sometimes doing it all is really self-serving, a fear of sharing the attention, rather than a true service to others. People genuinely enjoy helping in the kitchen, wrapping gifts, going to the post office, running out to get something you forgot. Let others be a part of the process of creating a Merry Christmas. Enjoy spotlighting their contributions and allow sharing the preparations to be part of Christmas joy.

Don't forget that a lot of love can sprout from a little in the world's perspective. The prophet Micah is the one who told us that the Messiah would be born in Bethlehem. (Micah 5:2) *But you, Bethlehem Ephrathah, though you are small among the clans of Judah, out of you will come for me one who will be ruler over Israel, whose origins are from of old, from ancient times.* This small town in Judah would be the birthplace of the Greatest Ruler ever known. As you are making all those preparations this Christmas, make sure to keep your candle of love burning bright.

25

Second Saturday in Advent
God's Amazing Love Makes You Wonder

It was Christmas Eve, 2004. My family and I were at our third church related event. My children used to lament being the children of two Christian counselors, now they know the woes of being the children of two ministers whom God called to two different churches. It was a lot of church, but that is what made the message of Christmas more poignant to me.

This day of three church-related events was not the most church I enjoyed that Christmas season. There were Christmas concerts at school and each church that we juggled to attend. What I am hoping to convey to you is the idea that I had been exposed to the Christmas story and the traditional Christmas passages not just on Christmas Eve, but during the entire Christmas season.

So it was me who was most surprised of all to hear the message of Christmas the way I did in my last Christmas service of 2004. The passage being read was Isaiah 9. It's my favorite part of Handel's Messiah. *For to us a child is born, to us a son is given.* I'm starting to sing it now.

Though I love that passage, I guess I have tuned out the last phrase of Isaiah 9:7. I never heard it like I heard it that Christmas Eve. *The zeal of the Lord Almighty will accomplish this.* Then it hit me: this is the message of Christmas. It is God's zeal for us that made Christmas happen at all. Christmas is all about the actions of a zealous God. He loved us so much that He made Christmas happen. As I sat in the pew I was revisited by the wonder of God's incredible love for me.

It was an amazing discovery that I had overlooked the entire Christmas season. Subconsciously, I thought my beautiful Christmas experience was because of me. I had considered the delight of my children in opening their gifts because we were able to locate everything on their lists. I'd thought about my own anticipation regarding Christmas—all the shopping, baking and decorating that I had offered to bring Christmas cheer to my family without complaining and in complete joy. I even complimented my husband on more than one occasion for his great attitude in putting up lights to share cheer with our neighbors and for helping me in the above tasks. What I had not considered was the zeal of the Lord that made Christmas happen. God is the creative force behind the creation of every good work in this world. His presence in the world has never been absent. His zeal for us causes Him to remain deeply involved in all the happenings of this world.

It is indeed the zeal of the Lord Almighty that has brought me into an eternal relationship with Him through the birth, death and resurrection of His Son. I'm delighted to be the object of His zeal. It is His zeal for me that gives me love at Christmas.

26

Third Sunday of Advent-Light One Candle for Joy
Shepherd's Candle

Light two purple candles and one pink candle: for Hope, Love and Joy
Sing: "While Shepherds Watched Their Flocks at Night" or "Silent Night"
Read: Luke 2:8-20 and Romans 15:13
Share: Who has brought you the most joy this Christmas?

Third Sunday of Advent

Light One Candle for Joy

In the season of advent, the candle of joy is the shepherd candle because the shepherds were overwhelmed by joy. My daughter says that the Shepherd candle is her favorite candle. It is the pink candle and highlights the joy of the season. Why is the third candle pink? Some say it signals the change in focus from repentance to anticipation of the second coming of Christ. Others say it is pink to remind us that Christmas is getting closer. Others wonder if one church accidentally ran out of purple candles and replaced a pink one which became a tradition. Just thinking of all the possibilities makes me smile. Joy is pink for me

When I think of joy in its purest sense, I think of new believers. They exude a glow that sparkles throughout their faces. The reality of their salvation through Christ can best be described as contagious joy. Joy is a gift from God. It results from knowing God. It doesn't come from our circumstances.

Paul was one of the most joyful apostles. His letter to the Philippians is all about the joy that became his through Christ. He told us to rejoice all the time. Philippians 4:4 says; *Rejoice in the Lord always, again I will say rejoice!* Paul's joy was apparent in very grim circumstances. He wrote the letter from his prison in Rome where he sat on death row. He definitely wasn't waiting for his wildest dreams to come true in order to find exuberant joy. Joy doesn't flow out of circumstances. Its source is much deeper than what is happening on the outside of us. In fact, the most joyful people I have met have overflowed in joy in spite of some of the most difficult circumstances.

During this season of Advent, we can receive the gift of joy or squelch its power to energize our Christmas. Joy is a gift from God, but we must take time to be with Him in order to receive the joy of knowing Him. You can't buy joy, you can't muster up joy. Real, genuine joy is a result of being loved by God. It is the fragrance of being in His presence.

In the busy Christmas shopping, baking, decorating, burning yourself out...you could use some real joy. Your shopping safari will turn into a joyful celebration when you spend time with God while you shop. Ask Him to help you find just the things you need at just the right prices. Invite His presence into your world of Christmas and be amazed by the joy it will bring into your life.

You may be like the shepherds, experiencing your same old day to day working environment. You are feeling just like last year, down to the wire and still a lot to do. Suddenly you become afraid. Afraid that Christmas will be here and will reveal what a failure you are at getting the right size, finding a beloved gift, not burning the Christmas dinner. When suddenly the message of Christmas bursts through into your life, you open your heart to the angel's message and you stop what you are doing and go to be with Jesus. After the shepherds saw Jesus, they didn't go back to their sheep watching life right away. They ran through the town of Bethlehem and shouted the good news to everyone they met. Jesus Christ is born!

Third Monday of Advent
Everyone Loves a Party!

Have you been attending Christmas parties? After a long day of work, you might have second thoughts about actually showing up. When you choose to attend anyway are you surprised that your dread soon turns to delight?

I don't think God is celebrating Christmas the way we do. But that's not because He doesn't love a party Himself. God is the one who instituted Festivals and Celebrations as well as Holidays for repentance and preparation. God is busy planning the ultimate party called the Bridal Feast of the Lamb. It's the celebration of the union of Jesus Christ and the church—all who have believed in Jesus while on earth. I don't know what the best party you have ever been to is, but this party will top all parties. It has been a long time in the planning so the experience of it will be figuratively and literally out of this world!

Have you ever felt awkward after mentioning a party to which someone wasn't invited? You don't have to worry about talking openly about this party because everyone is invited. There is no one who has ever been born who has not received a personal invitation to come to the party. Sadly, some will be too caught up in the measly offerings of this world while they live here and won't take the time to RSVP, and they will miss out on the greatest celebration in the universe and a whole lot more.

You don't even need to think about what to wear or what to bring to that party. All who are allowed to attend the party must be wearing Christ's robes of righteousness (Rev. 22:14). You need to make sure that you have received the robe. When you believe in Jesus as the Redeemer for your sins, you are automatically given this robe. You can't get into the party without it.

I can just imagine how it feels for God to go to all the preparation and all the effort to get ready for this party, but many won't be able to attend. There must be a sense of loss and sadness, but that never causes Him to ignore those of us who do desire to come near. When Jesus told the Parable of the Wedding Banquet, He ended with these haunting words, "*For many are invited, but few are chosen*" (Matt 22:14). That thought won't ruin the party, but it gives us something to think about. He will fill us with the joy of His presence and love. The party Host, the King of Kings and Lord of Lords, the Great I Am, will be the central beauty of the wedding feast. It will be so fulfilling to be in His presence taking in His glory and receiving His love. Every guest will feel just as special to the Host.

In the meantime, enjoy the parties you attend on earth. Drive safely and be careful on big party nights. Every time you get ready for a party on earth, consider the best party in the world, the one that will be thrown in heaven. Remember to tell everyone you know.

How are you looking forward to God's party?

Surprised by Joy

There are so many times in my life that I have been surprised by joy. One of the most vivid was the birth of my first child, Rachel. Her birth was a total surprise in that she was three weeks early. I was so excited to meet her; I remember telling the doctor in the office that day how anxious I was to hold this sweet baby. All the anticipation and expectation could not come close to what it felt like to actually deliver a healthy human being into the world. I just could not get over the fact that I had cooperated with God in this act of creating a new life, an eternal soul. I didn't even sleep one second for a 24 hour period; I was so overcome by joy.

I've been surprised by joy in hard times. I have experienced spiritual warfare in ministry that was taking down others who were ministering with me, but the more I submitted to God the greater joy I felt. I could not contain the joy. It made me feel sorry for the others who had to be around me because I knew misery loves company and I couldn't help the spiritual reality that was happening in my soul.

Joy is not the same as happiness; it is much deeper and much higher. It has nothing whatsoever to do with the circumstances you find yourself living through. Joy is catching a glimpse of heaven.

The shepherds were transformed on Christmas night into joyful bearers of good news all around the town of Bethlehem. Luke 2:16-18 describes their behaviors after they heard the news from the angels that Jesus was born: *So they hurried off and found Mary and Joseph, and the baby, who was lying in the manger. When they had seen him, they spread the word concerning what had been told them about this child, all who heard it were amazed at what the shepherds said to them.* The word "joy" is not mentioned as an adjective describing the shepherds, but their actions remind me of times of joy in my life, hurrying, seeing, spreading the word in a way that raises amazement in others. I wonder if the surprise visit on the hillside set them up for greater joy. Surprise is often linked to joy as well.

Recently I was surprised by joy when I followed God's instructions for beginning this Advent Season by rising before dark (Jesus' favorite time to pray) on Sabbath and spending time in quiet reflection. If you are finding yourself wishing for joy, let me tell you a guaranteed place you can find it. God says that you will be surprised by joy when you stop looking for joy in the things that please you. Isaiah 58:13-14 says, *If you keep your feet from breaking the Sabbath and from doing as you please on my holy day, if you call the Sabbath a delight and the Lord's holy day honorable, and if you will honor it by not going your own way and not doing as you please or speaking idle words, then you will find your joy in the Lord, and I will cause you to ride on the heights of the land and to feast on the inheritance of your father Jacob. The mouth of the Lord has spoken.*

Third Wednesday of Advent
God Is Born in the World of Men

This holiday season we focus on the fact that the God of the Universe humbled Himself to the point of becoming one of us. I could not state it more directly than Paul who wrote, "*Your attitude should be the same as that of Christ Jesus. Who being in very nature God, did not consider equality with God something to be grasped. But made himself nothing, taking the very nature of a servant, being made in the human likeness. And being found in appearance as a man, he humbled himself and became obedient to death—even death on a cross!*" (Philippians 2:5-8)

When Jesus was born He took on human nature. This actuality often goes unnoticed. We are so proud of our human flesh. We worship our bodies. But for Jesus, the state of being in human flesh was quite a demotion. We get a glimpse of how He really is at the transfiguration and in Revelation 1. Suffice it to say that He is magnificent. At Christmas He was born into our world. He came to the slums. He endured the smells and the darkness and the disasters because He loves us.

When Jesus grew older, He told us that we must be born again. Herein is another detail that gets too little recognition in our lives. The fact is that when we are born again we take on His divine nature. Mysterious as it sounds, God promises that we can be transformed from our sinful nature simply by believing that Jesus is Lord. This is the complete opposite of what Jesus experienced. Jesus was born into human flesh; we are born again into Divine Spirit. What a tradeoff! I actually become like Him. My whole DNA is transformed by becoming born again.

This explains the scriptures that state, "*For it is written: Be holy, because I am holy*" (1 Peter 1:16). God can have such high hopes for me because He has put Himself in me. I have been reborn, taking on His divine nature. What could I become if I let my rebirth take root and mature? God knows. He believes. He longs for me to fully embrace my heavenly nature.

When I stop and ponder what it means that Jesus was born into the world of men, I also reflect that I have been reborn in the world of God. These two births are completely incomprehensible, yet indispensable to relationship with God. I heard it put this way, Jesus became human so I could become Divine. If that doesn't bring joy, I don't know what will. It certainly is the source of joy for angels. Luke 15:10 describes the angels joy after reflecting the salvation of just one soul. *"In the same way, I tell you, there is rejoicing in the presence of the angels of God over one sinner who repents."*

This Christmas season we celebrate Jesus' birth, but also our own rebirth. Jesus glorified God by becoming a member of the human race. There is no greater joy you can bring to God than becoming a member of His heavenly Kingdom by being born again. Don't let another Christmas season pass without receiving your glorious destiny that Jesus' birth made possible. Jesus was born so that you could be born again.

Third Thursday of Advent
The Joy of Souls

Christ's coming to earth, taking on human flesh and living among us, leads a soul to feel its worth. The message in the lyrics of *O Holy Night* proclaim the spiritual transformation of Advent on the soul. Weary souls rejoice because Christ was born to be our friend through our trials. Souls are thrilled with hope because the sin and error can be redeemed.

My soul demands to be accepted, yet it receives condemnation, loved yet it is despised, valued though it is detested. In the fallen world in which I live, I receive contempt from the most unlikely of relationships. My soul cries out against this treatment. My soul detests these insults that it is powerless to defend. Are the burdens of life the reason for your soul's anguish? Does your soul demand to be loved, honored and cherished, yet receive so much less than what it was created to enjoy? Christ was born and the soul's worth is restored.

The birth of Christ resonates with my soul. The God of the universe coming to earth in the form of human flesh, so perfect and so helpless, nurtures the longings of my soul. The Christ child signals my soul's worth. Though my soul is wracked with sin and error, it still longs for holiness within and holiness in relationships with others.

The words of Jesus are the hope of all souls. Matthew 10: 28-31: "*Do not be afraid of those who kill the body but cannot kill the soul. Rather, be afraid of the One who can destroy both soul and body in hell. Are not two sparrows sold for a penny? Yet not one of them will fall to the ground outside your Father's care. And even the very hairs of your head are all numbered. So don't be afraid; you are worth more than many sparrows.*"

Advent transforms the soul through hope. When Christ was born, the soul received a Savior to cry its heart out. What brings the soul to tears now raises the soul to purpose. When Christ bears your burden, He reveals how it can bring about transformation. Jesus comes to comfort weeping souls and show them how to bear the cross of sorrow. He gives the strength to pick up the cross and hang on to the cross until the victory is experienced.

In Advent we examine the tears from our souls. We weep them into the arms of Jesus until we discover that He has a purpose for those tears. We become transformed, willing to accept the hurt, rejection, pain so that we can be like Christ—conquering all discomfort through picking up, hanging on and experiencing victory on the cross. In this way we are prepared to meet Jesus face to face when He returns. This is the spiritual work of Advent—preparing souls to meet Jesus.

How does Advent bring joy and anguish? What is the worth of your soul? As Christmas nears, is your weary soul rejoicing?

Third Friday of Advent
The Holiness of Love is Joy

Love is evidence of being created in the image of God. It is the remnant of our divine origins. God's love is the miracle that created Christmas. It was God's amazing love for us that prompted Him to send His only Son to us as a babe whose birth we celebrate at Christmas. It's the warmth of that love that we encounter during the season. In the midst of the black Friday brawls, there are amazing stories of strangers showing extraordinary love because God first loved us. Every time you encounter extraordinary love this Christmas, you encounter the holiness of the holiday. Love produces joy.

When we light the candle of joy, we acknowledge what the Shepherds observed in the Holy family. Mary's love for God motivated her to say "Yes" to the life-changing encounter with an angel and become the home for Jesus. Her love for God transformed her to love her Son, who became her Savior. It was Mary's joyful love for God that motivated her to say a wholehearted "Yes" to His invitation to become part of our redemption story.

Contrasting Eve and Mary reveals the holiness that leads to joy. Genuine love of God remakes us into holy people. Eve's unholiness began when she doubted God's goodness, while Mary's holiness abounded when she kept giving into her instinct to love and trust in God's good plan even when it made no sense to her. That is the power of placing your hope in God and trusting Him. It leads to joy.

A mother's love makes her most like God and causes her to reach beyond her own limits to respond to whatever her child may need. Mothers have a holy resilience when it comes to caring for their children. Mary showed that stamina of holy love when she stood by the cross while her Son hung in torment. Though that must have been the most horrific experience of her life, nothing could have taken her away from being beside the Son she loved. Love hurts but not enough to make us regret our love.

Love is what makes us better than we are. It is love that draws us to sacred, holy territory at Christmas. How can you move deeper into the love God pours into you through the Holy Spirit? Romans 5:5 says,

"And hope does not put us to shame, because God's love has been poured out into our hearts through the Holy Spirit, who has been given to us."

Here we see the connection between hope and love. Our hope is and has been God's love for us. His love is poured into our hearts through the Holy Spirit. The result is joy.

As we open our hearts to God's hope and love we become holy people. As we concentrate on God's goodness, we respond as joy-filled people. In the third week of Advent, take some time to connect to the hope, love and joy that has been poured into you by the Holy Spirit so that you find yourself pouring joy into others. This is sure to make your Advent a holy season.

How will you respond in hope, love and joy to whatever challenges you the most this Advent?

Third Saturday of Advent
Holy Joy!

How does joy become holy? If your joy is about having a certain experience, receiving a certain gift, getting a certain reaction, then you will or will not have joy based on whether your expectations are met. Presto-magic joy is achievable under certain circumstances.

Holy joy is an altogether different experience. If your joy is found in the thing that cannot be taken away from you, you can have joy in every circumstance you encounter this Christmas season. Let's say you are stuck in the airport for seventy-two hours while your dream Christmas melts away. That is definitely not a joyful thought. You are hungry, tired, broke, not to mention disappointed beyond measure. You can experience holy joy. This comes from making the object of your joy the reality that no matter how this situation plays out, you will be stretched and drawn closer to God through your prayers and hopes for the resolution you want and acceptance that His way has to be better even when you can't see it. It is totally possible to find joy in hardships.

Paul's most joyful letter to the church in Philippi was written from his prison cell—now that has got to be worse than missing days on your dream vacation and being stuck in the airport for 72 hours. I'm sure that Paul, being human, had a few tears and laments about his situation from time to time. Those releases led him to joy as he surrendered to whatever God had prepared for him. Holy joy cannot be created by human effort. It is the total surrender of trust and peace that God knows what He is doing and feeling blessed for what you have.

Sometimes it is hard to see the goodness you have been given when you feel like a prisoner in an airport. In fact, stopping to realize how much worse your situation could be is helpful toward moving into holy joy. When you feel like a prisoner, think about the innocent people who are literally prisoners, like Paul. Realize that your situation isn't as bad as it could be. Think about your fellow disappointed passengers and how some of them are dealing with health issues you are not, or others have a fear of flying which is being prolonged through the delay.

The birth of Christmas was full of joy. It was holy joy. There were tired pilgrims who were met with overcrowded accommodations forcing them to seek shelter in a cave used for animals. What joy they discovered when they could make the feeding trough—the manger—a cradle for their baby. The joy was shared when some dirty shepherds burst into their private place with tales of angels and directions and good news for all men. They found unexpected joy in the wrinkled faces of Simeon and Anna when they were privileged to see their Savior, for whom they prayed, as a baby. They likely felt joy when they realized the generous gifts they were given in Bethlehem by the Wise Men were exactly what they needed to sojourn in Egypt for the years they needed to be away until Herod the Great died. Psalm 16:11 reveals the source of joy: *"You make known to me the path of life; you will fill me with joy in your presence, with eternal pleasures at your right hand."*

Fourth Sunday of Advent-Light One Candle for Peace
Angel Candle

Light all four candles: for Hope, Love, Joy and Peace
Sing: "Angels We Have Heard on High" or "Hark the Herald Angels Sing"
Read: Luke 2:13-14 and Romans 5:1
Share: What does it mean to you that Christ's birth brought peace on earth?

Fourth Sunday of Advent
Light One Candle for Peace

Can you feel it? Do you have the peace of Christmas? Some might think a question like that is crazy to ask in the midst of the countdown to Christmas. Anxiety, yes, heartburn, occasionally, panic, almost, but peace...can't remember what that feeling is. The last candle of the advent is the angel candle because the angels' message was about peace on earth.

Luke 2:14 records what they told us: *"Glory to God in the highest, and on earth peace to men on whom his favor rests."* What is this peace about which the angels spoke? It is a peace that passes understanding. The peace on earth the angels promised is for here and now. Eventually, Jesus will return to earth and bring peace through creating a whole new heaven and earth minus Satan, demons and unrepentant men and women. That day will come. But, the peace is to all men now.

Have you ever experienced peace in your soul in spite of turbulent surroundings? That kind of peace is the mark of a favored Christian. Peace is a natural byproduct of being in touch with the truth that you are favored by God. I love this story of the Irish priest who went out into the rural parish. As he was walking, he passed an older peasant praying by the side of the road. The priest commented, "You must really love God." The peasant looked up and said, "Yes, he's very fond of me." Here was an old peasant man, with little to have peace from a materialistic perspective. But, peace doesn't come from what you own. You don't receive it from how many people you know. It isn't achieved by doing great things. Peace is the lasting knowledge that you are favored by God. If you have God's favor, then literally, what else could you need?

I won't be surprised if your overwhelming feeling isn't peace this close to Christmas. You are most likely still wondering if you can afford just one more present, or how you can make both of those parties in between the basketball playoff games. Yes, it is most hectic in your life right now. Still, you can have peace. Follow Philippians 4:6-7 and *"Do not be anxious about anything, but in everything, by prayer and petition, with thanksgiving, present your requests to God. And the peace of God, which transcends all understanding, will guard your hearts and your minds in Christ Jesus."* You can have peace. It comes through prayer. Why not pray about the things that you are anxious about right now?

You will light the candle of peace this Christmas not by never being anxious, but by praying about your anxieties. The flame of peace burns brighter with each prayer that you pray.

As Christmas draws closer and deadlines are more realistic, how are you being transformed spiritually by the peace that the angels announced?

List your anxious thoughts, then pray through each of them turning them over to God. Record how God answers your prayers.

36

Fourth Monday of Advent
Peace on Earth is God's Good Will Toward Men

I could be a multi-millionaire if I could find a way to bottle the peace that transcends understanding (Philippians 4:7). However, if I tried to do that, it would demonstrate that I didn't fully receive that peace. I only say it that way because it is a peace that is out of this world and something that lost souls are so desperate for that if they had even a taste of it, they would go to any extreme to have more of it. It is not something to be bottled and sold. It is offered to all for free.

I received this peace recently as an utmost gift from my loving God because He gives peace generously and unexpectedly to those who are seriously seeking Him. I got caught up in a conflict that got out of hand. Through prayer and wise counsel the Lord showed me my sin and asked me to confess what He showed me, and I did. The situation got worse; but this time (though I am not innocent for sure) I did not rebel against God and followed His direction to stand firm. When I came home I expected to be stirred up—I don't like to be involved in situations like this—but I was overcome with a supernatural experience of peace. I took that as God's delight in me, though fallen, I basically stood firm in a loving manner. The peace of earth the angels described to the shepherds in Luke 2:14 came to us from heaven in the form of the infant Jesus. Not only did I receive peace in my soul but I also felt good will toward those who stirred up the potential conflict. God's peace not only affects my relationship with Him; it also affects my relationship with others.

During this last week before Advent, we focus our hearts on the peace of the Nativity explained by God's messengers from heaven. These angels of Christmas are associated with the fourth candle of advent. While the prophets show us hope, Mary shows us love and the shepherds demonstrate joy; it's only a purely heavenly messenger that can tell us about peace.

Because of sin we have lost the peace of heaven. It can only be restored by repentance and obedience to the Christ child. I can't sell you that peace, but I can witness to it. Let me assure you that when you: *"Do not be anxious about anything, but in everything by prayer and supplication with thanksgiving let your requests be made known to God. And the peace of God, which surpasses all understanding, will guard your hearts and your minds in Christ Jesus"* (Philippians 4:6-7). you experience what the angels announced to the Shepherds—Peace on Earth.

Christmas Day is just around the corner. That is the day we light the white candle in the center of the Advent Wreath and receive the full glory of its light. It's all about the Christ child at Christmas.

Don't miss out on making time to reflect on God's greatest gift of the Christ child, especially now that the time is short. Remember how the virtues of hope, love, joy and peace have come to you this Advent Season.

Fourth Tuesday of Advent
The Candle of Peace Brings Greater Light

As we light all four candles of Advent we can't help but be reminded of the prophecy of Isaiah 9:2, *"The people walking in darkness have seen a great light; on those living in the land of deep darkness a light has dawned."* Jesus is the light, the first born of creation, foreshadowed in the first lights of creation (Genesis 1:3). On the fourth Sunday of Advent you light all four candles. The only time the light will be brighter is on Christmas day when you light all four candles and the white Christ Candle in the middle.

The fourth candle reminds us of the peace we now have with God because our Prince of Peace has come to us as Isaiah announced in Isaiah 9:6, *"For to us a child is born, to us a son is given, and the government will be on his shoulders. And he will be called Wonderful Counselor, Mighty God, Everlasting Father, Prince of Peace."*

During this last week of Advent we remember the peace that Jesus brought us. He brought us peace with God. Before His one and final sacrifice for sin there was no hope of eternal peace. Since He came to us as a babe in a manger, grew up and lived among us, He demonstrated in His life and teachings that He was indeed a Wonderful Counselor. His death and resurrection verified to us that He is Mighty God as that one act has the power to save the whole world from our sins. He showed us that He is our Everlasting Father and taught us how to see God as our Father and His Father. Jesus' purpose in coming to us was to make everything right and restore us to the peace we were created to enjoy. He is called our Prince of Peace.

Serenity is the cry of your soul. Although you live in a world torn apart by the realities of sin, you live with a God who brings you peace. There is a peace that passes understanding (Philippians 4:7). Do you know that peace? If you don't, what keeps you from lighting this forth candle of Advent, the candle of peace receiving the message the angels brought to the shepherds? When you let the light of Christ penetrate your darkness, you will find peace. You won't be able to explain what happened and why you are trusting God even though you can't see a way out of your problems, but you will be able to witness that there is a peace that doesn't make sense but is just as real as if it did. May your Christmas be blessed by receiving the Prince of Peace into your Christmas and into your life.

As you anticipate lighting the Christ candle on Christmas Day, remember that Jesus not only came once, but has promised to return for us. The Christ candle represents the true meaning of Advent–actively waiting for Christ to come back into our world, not as a suffering servant, but as the conquering hero. Christmas will soon come and go, but our waiting for Christ should be a year-round endeavor. Jesus last words to His disciples before He left this earth were about watching and waiting and expecting His return. You light the Christ candle when you commit to live your lives in anticipation of Jesus' return. Are you living the way you would like to be living when Christ returns for you?

Fourth Wednesday of Advent
Mary Was Ready for Christmas

You would think it would be easy for us to keep our focus on the wonderful spiritual breakthrough that began on the earth when Christ was born. Yet it seems more difficult than getting along with cranky relatives. The spiritual discipline of Advent was designed to help us grasp what is so easy to overlook at in our modern Christmas. We have some wonderful characters in the Christmas story that show us how to keep our hearts focused and prepared to let God touch us with profound spiritual realities and experience promised peace of the season.

The first character to receive the news that Christ was going to be born was Christ's mother, Mary. She had every excuse for not experiencing peace at Christmas. Unlike us, she was not accustomed to hearing the details of how Christ came to the earth from the Gospels. She had the concept that God was sending a Messiah, but she probably thought He would show up in Jerusalem around Passover. She was an ordinary girl. She was living an ordinary life. She was engaged to a wonderful man, and beginning to think about how to set up a home for the two of them. I'm sure that becoming the mother of her Savior was a notion she had never considered.

Into her ordinary life, an angel appeared and spoke to her about things too wonderful for her to fully comprehend. He began by telling her who she really is: *Greetings, you who are highly favored! The Lord is with you* (Luke 1:28). Perhaps this is the message you need to receive this Christmas. You need to know that you are highly favored by God and that He sent His Son to earth to die for you! You are the reason that Jesus was willing to leave heaven and enter this place that rejected and despised Him, so that He could save you. Maybe you need to stop and consider how God's messengers greet you this Christmas. Mary was a little taken back by this idea at first. But by Luke 1:48 she revealed that she fully accepted that she was favored by God. In her song she writes, "*For he has been mindful of the humble state of his servant. From now on all generations will call me blessed.*"

Mary not only received the message of who she really is to God, she also entered the mystery of what it means to walk with God. She managed to mutter one question, "*How can this be since I am a virgin?*" The angel answered her, but not with all the details. She knew that it had something to do with the Holy Spirit and the power of the Most High. That was all she needed to know. When a Holy and Infinite God is dealing with sinful and finite men and women, you have to accept that there is bound to be mystery. Mary asked a question and the angel offered an answer. To enter the spiritual realities of Christmas, you must be willing to accept the spiritual mysteries as well.

This is the wonder of Advent. We are all planning to have an ordinary Christmas. We are busy doing the ordinary chores that come with this season. Just like Mary, we too can be surprised by the Christmas message and accept it on a deeper level. That is the peace of Christmas.

Fourth Thursday of Advent
Waiting with Peace

In the best of times Christmas warms our hearts with peace. In the midst of the hustle and haggling of the season, even the news is peppered with nostalgic tales of loving-kindness expressed to strangers at Christmas. Hearts seem to grow warmer, not wanting anyone to miss out on the joy of feeling important during the Christmas season.

Mother Teresa said the greatest poverty in the world is the lack of love. Our world certainly can use all the love we have to give. Mary is a perfect example of human love. Her example calls us to the greatest love human hearts can hold. It is love of God. Mary demonstrated her love for God so fully in her response to the angel's bizarre assignment that she had been chosen to become the mother of Jesus. Unlike her Uncle Zechariah, she simply said, "*I am the Lord's servant.*" (Luke 1:38) Her childlike faith is anchored in her great love and trust in God. Daily, she had opened her whole heart, mind and spirit to God. She intuited that He is loving, good and kind, even if His ways were beyond her own understanding.

How much do you love God? Are you willing to risk it all out of love for Him like Mary? Are you willing to be embarrassed for Him? Is your love for God the driving force behind the reason you do what you do? There is no greater way to show your love for God than to give your will over to Him. Love for God is surrender.

Love for God is the most powerful emotion anyone can express. It is healing and gives healing to others. When we give our love fully and devotedly to God, as Mary did, our souls find our purpose.

As I wait for Christmas this advent, I am challenged by the weakness of my love. I know that I will never express the love I was created to know until I focus my love completely on God the way Mary did. Loving God transforms me. It gives me courage to do things for which I am not capable. It enables me to forgive, to wait, to believe, to hope.

As I wait for Christmas, I want to grow more and more in love with God who sent His Son Jesus to live as one of us, to die and to rise again so that our love can last for eternity. I want to love God above myself, my relationships, my dignity, my family, my future dreams just like Mary. Love for God and others leaves my soul in peace.

Fourth Friday of Advent
Repent, Change, Peace

How do you prepare for Advent? John the Baptist gave this advice: "*Repent, for the Kingdom of heaven is near*" (Matthew 3:2). Repent is a word with little appeal to our human nature. We don't know quite what God wants us to do. Does He want us to walk around in sackcloth and ashes? Should we sit around thinking about how much we sin until we cry? I think God is after a change of heart and Advent can help us get there.

What God wants most from us is that we change our mindset from the cares of this earth, to the wonder of His Kingdom. Advent heralds a change. It ushers in a renewed interest in God's Kingdom on earth. In Advent, there is often a change in seasons; we even get a little snow and ice in Dallas to escort in Advent once in a while. I change my closet and dig out my winter coat from the very back. The season of Advent invites us to change our focus from the everyday to the time when our Savior first came to us wrapped in cloths and lying in a manger.

That Advent two thousand years ago marks the preparation for the Kingdom of Heaven to arrive on earth. Our King was preparing to be born and finish His work of redeeming mankind by His sacrificial death. He now reigns in heaven until the time is just right for Him to return to earth and claim all citizens of heaven and earth to reign and rule with Him.

It's not easy to remain focused on the Kingdom of Heaven. It seems much less complicated to think about the bills to pay, the shopping and baking to do, the carpool to drive. All of these earthly concerns are in our face every day. It is a season, such as Advent, that causes us to stop and ponder the questions, *Why did Jesus come as a baby? What was God up to?*

There was a change in the world that occurred that wonderful day when Christ was born. God's redemption time clock was moving forward just as He had promised the prophets long ago. Advent reminds us that God did fulfill His promises and that He will continue to fulfill His promise of the earthly reign of Jesus Christ after His second coming to earth.

Advent asks me to open my heart to eternal destinies and heavenly promises. It calls me from the mundane work of living day to day to reconsider the Kingdom of Heaven and cry out to God to bring it to earth quickly. It encourages me by seeing that even after long centuries of waiting, God did fulfill His promises just like He said. It reminds me that there are still promises to be fulfilled.

In the meantime, I prepare by repenting; repenting of my puny view of my life and what I am here to do, repenting of being caught up in a worldly mindset that tells me a dream Christmas will satisfy my soul, repenting of spending too little time reflecting and meditating on the true meaning of Christmas.

I am mesmerized along with the shepherds by the promise of God for peace on earth. God says I am a citizen of the Heavenly Kingdom He has established on earth.

41

Fourth Saturday of Advent
Waiting with Peace

Deep breath—Christmas is here. Peace is in the air. The angels sang: *"Peace on Earth Good Will to Men."* They should know. Angels are messengers of God's peace. They bring the message without delay. The question is: Do we receive the peace the angels describe?

Peace in your soul evolves from a heart that has received the message of Christmas—that God gave His only Son to live, die, and rise again. This reality is what leads to peace. Peace is the destination we all desire in our souls. Advent paves a way to peace.

Peace begins when we hope in the promised Savior Whom the prophets foretold. A Savior taking on flesh to save the world can have no other motivation than pure love. The love of heaven to earth is unlike any other love. It is the love our hearts were created to enjoy. God proved His love for us through sending Jesus to us. He sent Him to become one of us. There is no greater love than taking on the sin of the entire world so that we can be saved through His righteousness. Hope and Love naturally lead to joy. The Gospel is joy given to the world. It is the too-good-to-be-true Good News! Who can contain the joy of a soul who comes to salvation through faith?

Advent brings us to peace this fourth week. We light the Angel Candle because the angels were the bearers of the good news: *"Glory to God in the highest heaven, and on earth peace to those on whom his favor rests"* (Luke 2:14.)

Their song is short and sweet yet penetrates the reality of a fallen world. The recipients of this undeserved favor will have hearts that glorify God and feel peace in the difficult circumstances of life. The angel's message contained news of great favor and ultimate peace. They were clear that this favor and peace should naturally lead to hearts that glorify God. If you know the peace the angels speak about, your heart will be full of praise and thanksgiving to God.

People who know me personally know that my circumstances are full of challenges and heartbreaking realities. If I did not have the peace of God, I think I would be sitting in the back of my closet in the fetal position paralyzed by the harsh realities of my life. Perhaps I'm being a little dramatic, but my life experiences could overwhelm me, if it were not that I know what the peace of God can do. When I recognize that the hard things I am facing are not punishment from God rather opportunities to grow in faith, my soul opens to deeper spiritual experiences. The peace I have cannot be found anywhere on earth. It comes directly from heaven. The peace on earth will literally come in the future when Jesus comes the second time and remakes the heavens and the earth. In the meantime, peace on earth can only be experienced inside the hearts of individuals who put their hope, love and joy in the work of the baby who came at Christmas, then lived, died, was buried and rose again and now lives in heaven interceding for us.

December 25-The Nativity of Our Lord: Christmas Day

Today and today only, you light the white candle in the middle of your Advent Wreath. It is the Christ Candle.

Read Luke 2:1-7

Are you ready for Christmas to be over, or are you dreading the regular days that lay ahead, packing up all the fun of Christmas and wishing the joy could last all year? Christmas comes with tons of obligations, expectations and surprises. What happened in your soul on Christmas day? You can capture some of the moments of Christmas by doing this Christmas Day examen.

1. What moment of Christmas Day brought you the most love?

2. What moment of Christmas Day brought you the least love?

3. What do you need to remember about the Christmas season this year that you want to repeat or avoid for next year?

Christmas Season begins on Christmas Day. In the west, liturgical churches acknowledge the twelve-day festival, starting on December 25 and ending on January 5. It is known as Christmastide, Christmas Season, or the twelve days of Christmas. This is the season between the Feast of the Nativity (Christmas Day) and the Feast of Epiphany (January 6---celebrating the visit of the Magi). Though Advent is over this devotion will focus on the 12 Days of Christmas as a season of spiritual reflection and renewal. It will guide you to consider the experiences you have lived this past Christmas and Holiday season and help you digest the lessons you have learned.

During these twelve days, the calendar will change. You will have a whole new year ahead of you. It's a perfect time to spend extra focus on your soul and ways you can live each day of the new year with purpose and meaning. The church Father's created the Church calendar as a tool of discipleship. I've found the seasons and organization draws my mind back to reflect on Christ and then the purpose of my life. I want each day of this year to be a day that I live fully and connect to God's plan for my life.

Ephesian 2:10 says: *"For we are God's handiwork, created in Christ Jesus to do good works, which God prepared in advance for us to do.* The year ahead has been thought about by God. He has prepared in advance for every challenge, joy, loss, gain that we have yet to learn about.

December 26—Saint Stephen Feast Day

Following the Church Calendar, Saint Stephen's Feast day is the day after Christmas. I wonder why the church father's put this day in the middle of the focus of Jesus' birth. Stephen was the first martyr of the Christian church. His Feast Day is a somber celebration of the truth that a life lived well for God does not necessarily mean a life without tragedy. I'm sure they have a good reason for choosing December 26th.

For most Americans December 26th is the first day to flock to the malls and exchange gifts that don't fit or you just don't like. In England, it is known as Boxing Day—a holiday giving household servants the day off after they worked so hard for their families on Christmas day.

What lessons can we learn by reflecting on St Stephen? If you go to Jerusalem today the Lion's gate where his stoning took place is still in use. Christian's call it the Stephen Gate, while it is known as the Lion's Gate to Jews and Muslims. Stephen didn't live to be an old man, yet his life never be forgotten because of how he lived and how he died. He was described as a man full of "*God's grace and power*" (Acts 6:8). We are told he did many miraculous works and that the educated Jews could not argue against his wisdom. Rather, they spread lies about him and stirred up a crowd to stone him.

You can find his beautiful wisdom recorded in Acts 7 as he answered the question asked by the priest at his inquisition. It is a beautiful summary of the work of God prior to and through sending Jesus Christ to live, die and rise again.

As the furious men with murderous hearts starting heaving their stones, Stephen looked up and saw Jesus standing at the right hand of God. *But Stephen, full of the Holy Spirit, looked up to heaven and saw the glory of God, and Jesus standing at the right hand of God. "Look," he said, "I see heaven open and the Son of Man standing at the right hand of God"* (Acts 7:55-56). In almost every Orthodox church you will see an icon of Jesus captured in the blue of the sky to represent the sight Stephen described. Acts 7 gives the first mention of the apostle who would go on to write half of the New Testament and even bring the writer of Acts to Christ: Paul. Not yet converted, Paul stood there watching over the coats of the men who were killing Stephen.

Though Stephen's martyrdom was a crippling blow to the small church and all who loved him, it was critical to the spread of the Gospel throughout the world. Because of his death many believers fled Jerusalem and began their assignment of bringing the gospel to the whole world.

Reflection:
What have been the three worst events in your life?

What have you learned about God and how have your grown spiritually through them?

December 27- Saint John Feast Day

John the Evangelist called himself the Beloved. The Gospels witness about his spiritual growth from the duo who Jesus nicknamed "Sons of Thunder" (John and his brother James) to being known as the disciple whom Jesus loved. He not only knew that he was loved by God, he wrote that each of us are as loved by God in 1 John 3:1: *See what great love the Father has lavished on us, that we should be called children of God! And that is what we are! The reason the world does not know us is that it did not know him.*

John Piper was inspired to write the entire book, <u>The Pleasures of God</u> after reading this statement by Henry Scougal: 'The worth and excellency of a soul is to be measured by the object of its love." The quote inspired Piper to consider the object(s) of God's love.

The object of God's love is Jesus Christ and the object of Jesus' love is God the Father. There is nothing Jesus wants more for us than to become a part of this kind of soul-satisfying love.

Jesus' desperate desire for us to know our true love was a part of His great interceding prayer for all believers in John 17:26: *I have made you known to them, and will continue to make you known in order that the love you have for me may be in them, and that I myself may be in them.*

Jesus prays that He will be the object of this love. He prays that we will have the same kind of love that the Father has for Him. If this was anyone else praying this prayer, we would be appalled at the audacity of the thought. We would think, this guy is praying that I will love him the way his Father loves him. How self-centered can that be?

Yet, it is not self-centered at all. We were created to love God. One of the most important ways we can display our love for God is to love His Son. When we love Jesus, we are loving God. It was hard for God to contain His love for Jesus; three times the gospels record His shout from heaven: This is my Son in Whom I am well pleased! When was the last time you wanted to shout about how much you love Jesus? Does your love for Jesus move you more than your love for others?

I confess; I do love Jesus. But I don't love Him like God does. I haven't given Him the name that is above every name (Philippians 2:9). I give Him my consideration in my daily quiet time. I'm surprised by Him when I'm not looking. I'm comforted by Him. I rely on Him for my salvation and for my righteousness. But, I don't come anywhere close to loving Him the way God loves Him. What would happen in my life if I loved Him the way God loves Him?

As I consider the object of my love, I have to say that Jesus often takes second place to my love for myself, my children or my friends. What would happen in my life if I truly focused on the love God has for Jesus and craved that same love to be in me? As you go through this day, consider the object of your love and strive to see Jesus' prayer answered in your life – that you could love Jesus with the same love that God has for Him.

December 28—The Holy Innocents
Suffering Is Part of the Story

The news is full of reports of human suffering in your community and around the world. Hurricanes, earthquakes, wars, human tragedies devastate this world. The feast of the Holy Innocents memorialized Herod's satanic act of slaughtering innocent babies in an effort to kill Jesus (Mt 2:16-18).

Jesus seemed to embrace His suffering. The disciples had all come on board. They had been with Him through the good times, feeding of 5000, hundreds of healings, great teaching, and silencing the religious leaders. It was time for Jesus to ask them the golden question. He asked them straight out. "But what about you?" he asked. *"Who do you say I am?" Peter answered, "God's Messiah."* (Luke 9:20).

That's great. That's important. You must get this fundamental fact down before you are ready to handle the rest of Jesus' story. Jesus is the Christ of God, the Son of God. Have you come to know and understand that fact yet? When you do, you are ready to understand more.

He told them *"The Son of Man must suffer many things and be rejected by the elders, chief priests and teachers of the law, and he must be killed and on the third day be raised to life"* (Luke 9:22). In the same lesson about knowing Who Jesus is, the disciples were also taught that being the Son of God meant embracing suffering. Jesus seems to connect being the Son of God with the mission of the Son of God. Who He was and what He must do seemed to fit nicely together in Jesus' mind.

Many of us do not feel very chosen by or close to God when we are faced with suffering. In fact, we might be known to make some horrible accusation about God when we are in pain. We feel that God has slighted us by not protecting us from the pain that overwhelms our lives. For Jesus, this was not the case. It was definitely because He was the Son of God that the fact of suffering did not unnerve Him. The fact that He would have to suffer the most immense kind of suffering any human being has ever known did not make Him question whether He was the Son of God or whether God loved Him.

The suffering was a part of His purpose on earth. He didn't like it. He didn't look forward to it. But, He was sure that it would need to happen.

Suffering was part of Jesus' story. He told them plainly, now that you know that I am God's Son I have more to tell you about myself. I am God's Son and I will suffer. I will be rejected and killed, and on the third day raised to life. This is all part of my journey. I want you to know that I am not afraid of My suffering, I accept My suffering. That doesn't make it any less painful, but it does make it have a purpose in my life

What suffering has God asked you to accept?

How can you make your suffering less?

December 29
Three Questions for Christmastide

Christmas is over. The climatic hustle of the Western world has descended to the natural outcome of gifts exchanged, swelled stomachs, and wearied travelers destined to face the unalterable fact that there is an inescapable void from living in a fallen world even with all the promises that Christmas is the most wonderful time of the year.

Facing the complex reality of living in a fallen world is a perfect opportunity to face that void within and ask yourself some important spiritual questions, these questions have the potential to restore your soul and set you on track spiritually to live out the true promises of God.

God, who is your Creator, is your Provider and Protector. He defends and befriends you and gives you this pattern from the beginning of His Word. He created the world and provided everything human beings would need to live within it, including the warning not to eat of the Tree of the Knowledge of Good and Evil—one command. Even after sin, God defends us by giving us gifts we need to live in a fallen world. He gives us the gift of tears to cry out the poison that infiltrates our souls. He tells us to take a Sabbath to re-orientate our souls as to Who He is. He sent His Son to die for our sins and by the power of His blood it is possible for us to overcome the sorrows associated with living in this world of woes. He gives us His Word filled with His commands.

Even before sin He offered commands for living in Paradise. There are five commands found in Genesis 2:28: 1. Be fruitful 2. Multiply 3. Replenish the earth—replace what you use up 4. Subdue it 5. Have dominion over the fish of the sea and over the fowl of the air, and over everything that moves on the earth.

All Christians are capable of bearing spiritual fruit such as love, joy and peace. We are sent out with this fruit to disciple and teach others to disciple. We are asked to consider what we received when we were born into this fallen world and how our lives can make the world better in some ways before we leave here through our death. Christians must subdue the world and push back the effects of the fall through the fruit they bear when they do not compromise the truth of God's word even when people will not listen. Christians are commanded to take dominion over sin by not compromising His word with the world's values.

We can live out these commands by asking ourselves the three spiritual questions that keep us on track with God's purposes.

- **Who am I?** You are a dearly beloved child of God.
- **What am I to do with my life?** Live it in preparation for your death by following God's will for your life.
- **How am I to do it?** Meditate on God's word and be guided by the Holy Spirit as to the ways you specifically live out your days.

The fact is our life here on earth has a purpose:
For we must all appear before the judgment seat of Christ, so that each of us may receive what is due us for the things done while in the body, whether good or bad (2 Corinthians 5:10).

December 30
He Will Make All Things New!

I just love a New Year. It seems to bring with it a sense of hope that everything that went wrong in the year before no longer exists, and I can move forward fresh and clean with no mistakes, mishaps or misfortunes.

Is it possible to become so eager for something new that I discard something valuable? I began to question this after what I did. For months, an ugly calendar hung on the side of my refrigerator. It is not a calendar that I keep important dates, rather one that offers reference to the time and place when I am in the kitchen. Last year, we forgot about this calendar and we ended up using the back page of the one from the year before. It wasn't a solution I particularly liked, but it did the job and I was not industrious enough to do anything else about it.

When December 31st arrived, I made a decision. That calendar was coming down. I would at least replace it with something that changed each month. I pulled it off my refrigerator and looked over its garden scenes from the year before noting how beautiful they were and wondered why I didn't appreciate it more. Wishing for a calendar like that old one, I grabbed one that came in the mail for free and put it up, prepared for January 1.

On New Year's morning my husband noticed that I was ahead of the game for the year and had already changed the calendar. He asked, *What did you do with the calendar that was there?* I told him I threw it away the day before. That's when he explained that he had bought a new calendar months ago that started with the remaining months of the year. I had thrown away a brand-new calendar filled with garden scenes he picked out just for me.

We went outside to the trash bin and searched for the calendar. It was bent and crumbled, but salvageable to use for this New Year. Presently it is being pressed under some heavy books, but eventually I will pull it out and hang it on my refrigerator. Its creases will remind me, not to throw out what was important from the past.

God doesn't throw out what is old to make it new. He didn't destroy the world when Adam and Eve sinned. He didn't completely destroy the world when He was forced to begin anew with Noah and his family. He makes us new from the material we are before Him. Colossians 3:10 says, *and have put on the new self, which is being renewed in knowledge in the image of its Creator.* We all want a new self for the New year, but remember that God will renew all that we have experienced, including, mistakes, mishaps and misfortunes. All we have experienced has the potential to be renewed, bringing us deeper into the knowledge of God and closer to the image we bear of His likeness. God makes things new without discarding any parts of you. I like the way Eugene Peterson paraphrases Colossians 1:3 in the Message. *Now you're dressed in a new wardrobe. Every item of your new way of life is custom-made by the Creator, with his label on it.* Enjoy the process of being renewed in the coming year!

December 31
The Secret to Life

James Taylor said that *the secret to life is enjoying the passage of time*. He felt that *any fool can do it; there ain't nothing to it* (James Taylor, Secret 'O Life). I'm not sure if I agree that there's really nothing to it, but I do believe that there is something very important in this life to appreciating the meaning of time and discovering how to fully enjoy it. Time is something we experience on this universe. Happiness has something to do with connecting to the eternal and acknowledging that time is temporal. Jesus came to offer life and offer it more abundantly (John 10:10), that abundant life is eternal life. Our life on this earth is only abundant when we understand how it relates to eternity.

I believe the concept of time in heaven is very distinct from what we experience on earth. I don't think our loved ones could be happy in heaven if they were still trapped by time, ticking off the seconds until the ones they love are out of their pain. I believe that even if they can see us living our lives, they take it in with a knowledge we don't possess, and see our experience of time with divinely inspired eyes.

So what is the secret to enjoying the passage of time? Haven't the happiest times in your life been when you've become unconscious of time? That was a little taste of heaven. How long is ten minutes when you are waiting in the Doctor's office to find out the diagnosis after your biopsy? How long is a toothache, or a traffic jam? It was probably at the moments that you were most unaware of the passage of time that you have enjoyed the most. That's when you were experiencing a taste of eternity. It could have been as simple as enjoying an evening of rich conversation with an old friend.

You can either look at your life as a never ending coach flight across the Atlantic seated near the restroom, or you can sit back and begin a meaningful conversation with the young man sitting to your left. What you do with your time makes all the difference.

We were not made for time, but for eternity. So, yes James Taylor, the secret of life is enjoying the passage of time. And how do you do that? It's really quite difficult, but true that any fool can do it. You enjoy the passage of time most fully when you gain an eternal perspective. Even if you are living right in the middle of the most difficult moments of time you have ever experienced, you can enjoy time by remembering you are just passing through.

Time is not eternity. God has set limits on our suffering. He has given us a timed test; it is our lives. We can see our whole existence as a test of whether we learn the secret to life. Matthew 6:19, 20 says, *Do not store up for yourselves treasures on earth, where moth and rust destroy, and where thieves break in and steal. But store up for yourselves treasures in heaven, where moth and trust do not destroy, and where thieves do not break in and steal.* Use your time storing up heavenly treasures and you will have learned the secret of life.

January 1- The Holy Name

God is the one who told the angel to tell Mary to name His Son Jesus. Jesus is the one who taught us to think of God as our Father. God gave this image of Himself with mankind in the Old Testament (Deuteronomy 1:31; Psalm 103:13; Malachi 3:17) but it was not until Jesus that we began to comprehend that God wants us to think of Him as our Father during prayer. I love that Jesus didn't teach us to pray to His Father. Jesus calls God our Father. Jesus called Him Abba—Daddy. When we pray we are to consider that we are talking to our Father, He is the Father to the fatherless. No Father compares to God as our Father. Jesus delights in sharing His special relationship with His Father (Matthew 6:6) and encouraging us to address the Almighty God, the Creator of the Universe, the Most Holy of All; Father.

Once we grasp that we are speaking to Our Abba-Father, we recognize that He is in heaven—*Who art in heaven.* Jesus asks us to center our prayer by grasping the reality of heaven even while we pray from earth. Heaven should be on our mind each day and throughout the day. Heaven is our hope. It is our goal. It is the place we want to be after God determines that our time on earth is finished. If we think of heaven every day, we won't get so caught up in the constant worries and concerns of the world. Heaven is what centers us to live into the fullness of God's will for our life on earth. The heavens that we see with our eyes remind us that Our Father is in heaven (a place more wonderful than we can imagine) preparing a place for us so that we can be with Him there. Heaven is a real place. Heaven is where God is. We don't learn of heaven by limiting our knowledge to the out-of-body recollections that people have described when they die and come back to life. We learn about the place of heaven by the descriptions that God has given us in the Bible. It is the place He wants us to be. It is a place that no one visits and comes back to earth. Paul said he went there (he wasn't sure if it was in the body or in a trance, 2 Corinthians 12:2) but he wasn't allowed to write what he saw. He was eager to go there permanently (2 Timothy 4:8). John wrote of heaven in some degrees in Revelation and he too informed us that some things he was not permitted to write (Revelation 10:4).

Hallowed be Thy Name is the response to forming the concept that we are praying to Our Father in Heaven. It is by His grace that we can call Him by a name. That name has power beyond our imagination. We are transformed by calling on His name. When we are lifting up His name we are doing the opposite of sinning, we are halting the rebellion that comes naturally to us and acknowledging that His Name is holy, honored and wonderful. The original sin of doubting God's goodness is transmuted. Isaiah 43:21 says: *The people I formed for myself that they may proclaim my praise.*

We were created for this very purpose to give praise to His holy name. It is indeed our honor and our dignity that we repeat this first phrase. We orient ourselves to the great and beautiful God who is our Father in heaven whose name is above all and amazing beyond words.

January 2
Good, Pleasing and Perfect Will

Discovering God's will is interesting to most people. We would like to consider what God's will is for our lives and decide if we want to follow it. We find doing His will compelling in some ways and terrifying in other ways. The truth is that most of us don't wake up each morning with the thought: I wonder what God's good, pleasing and perfect will is for me today!

The reason for that can be deduced from Romans 12:1-2, *"Therefore, I urge you, brothers, in view of God's mercy, to offer your bodies as living sacrifices, holy and pleasing to God—this is your spiritual act of worship. Do not conform any longer to the pattern of this world, but be transformed by the renewing of your mind. Then you will be able to test and approve what God's will is—his good, pleasing and perfect will."*

The reason we don't think of God's will as good, pleasing and perfect is probably because our minds are focused on a different definition of good, pleasing and perfect. That should be freeing news in some ways. It's not that God's will is something to be feared; it is that God's will is something that requires the right kind of mind—one that is not conformed to this world.

You might think that loving God's will means loving God. That is not necessarily true. You can believe God, love God and even believe He cares for you and not love His will if you haven't loved Him with all your mind. Loving God with all your heart is believing God is good, loving and kind. Loving God with all your mind is believing God is good and His ways are good.

Thomas Keating says, "...the prayer of the day asks that we be shown, the good, the acceptable, and the perfect will of God. This prayer suggests that there are three degrees of submission to the will of God. The good will of God is the will above every other affection. And the perfect will of God is his will above every other love including ourselves." [1] Keating didn't make a suggestion about the acceptable will of God. I might add the acceptable will of God is when we respond to His will above our own will. We can only fully accept God's will when our minds are transformed enough to believe His will is perfect and good.

If you are having trouble knowing the will of God, turn your attention to knowing the goodness of God. Your mind won't accept what it doesn't believe to be good. Oh that we could all honestly pray the prayer of St. Francis:

God:

I offer myself to Thee to build with me and to do with me as Thou wilt.

Relieve me of the bondage of self that I may better do Thy will.

Take away my difficulties so that victory over them may bear witness to those I would help.

Of Thy power, Thy love and Thy way of life, may I do Thy will always.

AMEN.

January 3—Rich Welcome

Have you ever received a rich welcome? I can think of many welcomes I have encountered. I have received dutiful welcomes—you know the kind where the person is forced to allow you into their home either from some kind of business or family obligation. The door opens to you; you are not blocked from entrance, but you know that you are really not wanted. No one is really excited that you have finally arrived, in fact the homeowners are more likely looking forward to the end of your visit than they are to your arrival. I have received a warm welcome, the kind where someone is very touched that you have come into their world. That person is happy to see you come and sad when you must leave. I have met startled welcomes and shy welcomes. I have contended with an unkind welcome when someone has literally slammed the door in my face, but I can't say that I have received the kind of welcome that Peter says God longs to give me when I reach heaven. Peter describes what is on God's mind. He hopes to be able to give me a rich welcome. I can't wait to see what God has in mind.

In my mind, a rich welcome would be coming into a place where everything that is important to me is stocked to overflowing. The people I love, the experiences I treasure, the food I enjoy; all laid out to please me. There would be beaches with dolphins laughing and playing, mountains filled with wildflowers with gentle horses to ride, hiking trails filled with butterflies; waterfalls leading to tepid pools for swimming and rapids to traverse. I would love fresh picked blueberries and Danish lobster tails with melted butter. I could go on and on imagining what a rich welcome might involve.

I have no idea what God might have in mind for a rich welcome, but Peter claims that I can be sure to receive it—if! 2 Peter 1:10-11 states: *Therefore, my brothers and sisters, make every effort to confirm your calling and election. For if you do these things, you will never stumble, and you will receive a rich welcome into the eternal kingdom of our Lord and Savior Jesus Christ.*

Although I will need to wait until heaven to discover if I get a rich welcome and what a rich welcome might contain; living my life so God can give me a rich welcome will be evident in my life now. Confirming my calling and election through walking in virtues guarantees that I will not be defeated existing this fallen world. When I live into my divine nature as evidenced in the virtues of faith, goodness, knowledge, self-control, godliness, brotherly kindness and love, my life here on earth is satisfying. Peter wants me to consider how much this way of life will bless me, not only in this life, but in the life to come. Someone descried it: **Living your life to put a smile on the face of God.**

This is my focus for the new year. I want to be eager and determined to live out the gift of the divine nature via exhibition of the above-mentioned virtues and even more. My life here on earth is so short in light of eternity, yet how I live it will affect how I will experience eternity.

January 4
Have You Gotten Your Passion On Purpose?

Socrates said, "The unaware life is not worth living." Yet, that is the way most of us spend each day. By that I don't mean that we live a day without being in touch with reality. Rather, for most of us, we spend our days so much in touch with real life that we end up living unaware lives.

What I have found is that if I don't take time to become aware of my life, I end up doing lots of important things, but not the things that are important to Jesus.

The idea of living a passion on purpose first knocked me into awareness in 1994. It was after a trip to Europe. The Berlin Wall had fallen and all everyone in Europe was talking about was the Euro. American media wasn't even covering the historical issue of common currency. I wasn't a devout student of Revelation, but the signs were definitely pointing to the one world government. I had to stop and ponder; what if Jesus were to come back in the year 2000? I wrote a list of things that I thought God would want me to be doing.

When I started writing the book Passion on Purpose, I found the scribbled note I had written so many years ago. I was surprised to find that many of the items on my list matched with the study of God's word I was doing in order to write the book. It was very encouraging. Is pleasing Jesus a thought when you make plans for how to live your life?

1. Jesus gives heavenly reward to those who use their financial resources for His kingdom (Matt. 6: 19-21).
2. Jesus gives rewards for the spiritual disciplines we practice with the right motives (Matthew 5-8, 16-18; 1 Corinthians 9:17; 1 Corinthians 4:5)
3. Jesus gives rewards for standing up for your faith (Matthew 5:11-12; Luke 6:22-23; Revelation 2:10; James 1:12).
4. Jesus gives rewards for the way you treat others (Matthew 10:40-42; Luke 14:12; Hebrews 6:10; 1 Thessalonians 2:19-20; Mark 9:41; Luke 6:32-35)
5. Jesus gives rewards for dedicating everything you do to glorify God (Colossians 3:23-25, Romans 12:1).
6. Jesus gives rewards for keeping God's Word pure (2 John 7-8; Revelation 2-3).
7. Jesus gives reward for being watchful for His return (2 Timothy 4:8; Luke 12:35-48; Mark 13:32-37).

Brennan Manning challenges us to think about our lives. He writes; "The paltriness of our lives is largely due to our fascination with the trinkets and trophies of the unreal world that is passing away. Sex, drugs, booze, the pursuit of money, pleasure and power, even a little religion, suppress the awareness of present risenness. Religious dabbling, worldly prestige, or temporary unconsciousness cannot conceal the terrifying absence of meaning in the church and in society, nor cans fanaticism, cynicism, or indifference." (Brennan Manning, Abba's Child, Navpress, p. 120)

January 5—The Gift of the Magi

We think of the Magi as three wise men who traveled from Africa to honor the birth of the King of the Jews. We really don't know how many magi there were, only that three gifts were presented. The scripture merely informs us that they were from the East, although they most likely traveled out of Africa first to Jerusalem, then to Bethlehem.

What else we discover about the Magi lingers by reading between the lines of their short story in the Bible recorded only in Matthew 2:1-13. These thirteen verses help us learn from their lives. First of all, they were curious about spiritual things. It's doubtful that they made regular treks chasing kings. This was most likely a once in a lifetime journey. They seemed to be focused on this one king. They didn't have the writings of the prophets; else they would have gone directly to Bethlehem, rather than Jerusalem where they met King Herod. God reveals Himself in His creation, through the prophets and in the last days through His Son Jesus Christ as well as in our hearts. Though they didn't have all the facts when they left on their journey, along their way they learned more about the king whose special star appeared to announce his kingship. God spoke personally to them through His creation (the star), the prophets (visit to Jerusalem), worshipping Jesus Christ, and in their hearts (dream).

Have you seen the plaque that says, "If it had been three Wise Women instead of three Wise Men, they would have asked directions, arrived on time, helped deliver the baby, cleaned the stable, made a casserole, and, brought practical gifts?"

It might be a funny joke, but it is not necessarily biblical. The wise men did ask for directions and brought very practical gifts. I can't presume too much about cleaning the stable, helping to deliver the baby, arriving on time, or making a casserole.

These Wise Men have a lot to teach us about pursuing God discovering Jesus. These men were wise by earthly standards. They were known by those in their community as men of knowledge. They knew more than the common man about the stars, government and worldly matters. But that is not what made them wise.

The Wise Men were wealthy. They had the wisdom to earn and invest money in such a way that they could lavish expensive gifts on strangers and make long, costly journeys to distant lands. This was most uncommon for the overwhelming majority of the inhabitants of the world at that time.

By far the wisest reality they taught us is found in Matthew 2:11: "*On coming to the house, they saw the child with his mother Mary, and they bowed down and worshiped him.*"

The last record we have of the Magi concerns them hearing from God and obeying God in Matthew 2:12: "*And having been warned in a dream not to go back to Herod, they returned to their country by another route.*"

The Maji bring you and me the great gift of showing us how to pursue God and find Him!

January 6—The Feast of the Epiphany

Today is Epiphany. On January 6 the church celebrates the Feast of Epiphany. Protestants don't normally think about it; the Western church attaches Epiphany to the Wise Men who searched out Jesus after His birth. The Eastern church focuses on the baptism of Jesus when He was revealed as the Son of God as the Epiphany.

For me it has become the day that I finally turn off the Christmas lights that have brightened the dark world during the Christmas season. After all the effort to get them up, I hate to take them down right after Christmas. I wait the full twelve days after Christmas until Epiphany to carry out the sad but by now much needed task. After all, I say I put them up partly as my Christmas Greeting to my neighbors. I think they are very tired of them by January.

Of all the events in Jesus' life that we celebrate, this one may seem the least important. One may wonder why it got priority on the church calendar in light of more important happenings (like the calling of the disciples) that do not have their own feast day.

I'm glad that I have Epiphany to think about the Magi who traveled to worship Jesus. Immersed within the birth, ministry, and death of Jesus, Gentile interactions pop up. The Magi are the first Gentiles to worship the one true King of all time. They thought they were coming to celebrate the King of the Jews, but they discovered a connection to the God of the Universe. They certainly had a true epiphany.

As I take down my Christmas lights, I use Epiphany to reflect on what the Advent and Christmas season has meant to me this year. I treasure my memories as I put away another Christmas season. I will never come to fully comprehend all that God did for me at Christmas. I certainly don't have the desire nor the insight to figure out anything that God has hidden in the stars—I have a hard time finding the big dipper and the little dipper way up there. No, I'll spend my efforts concentrating on how to wind up the lights so that the right end is ready to connect for the next Christmas.

What I can immolate from the Wise Men is the worship of Jesus Christ the New Born King. I can stop on this day and behold Him by considering all that He came to this earth to do for me then and how much He does for me now from His seated position at the right hand of God.

After all my gifts from Christmas are all put away, now I can think about Jesus the way the Magi show me. Matthew 2:11 says, *"On coming to the house, they saw the child with his mother Mary, and they bowed down and worshiped Him. Then they opened their treasures and presented Him with gifts of gold, frankincense and myrrh."*

I'll let this day remind me to bow down and worship Jesus and bring Him the gift He most desires: my surrendered and humble heart.

What have been your epiphanies from celebrating the 12 days of Christmas?

Recipes

White Chocolate Popcorn
1 24 oz. package of white almond bark (sometimes called white bark, sometimes called white almond bark, sometimes called white chocolate bark) – the kind I buy comes with 12 squares per package
3 bags of microwave popcorn

Pop one bag of popcorn and remove all unpopped kennels. Melt 1/3 package of bark according to package directions. Mix with popcorn. Spread on cookie sheet and let dry. Repeat with other 2 bags of popcorn.

Christmas Sugar Cookies
1 cup butter or margarine softened
1 ¾ cups powdered sugar
1 egg
2 teaspoons vanilla extract
Finely grated rind of 1 lemon
2 tablespoons lemon juice
2 ½ cups all-purpose flour
1 teaspoon baking soda
¼ teaspoon salt
For Icing:
2 ½ cups powdered sugar
¼ teaspoon cream of tartar
2 large egg whites
Food coloring

Cookies
Cream butter and 1 3/4 cups powdered sugar until light and fluffy. Beat in egg, vanilla, lemon rind, then lemon juice. Add flour, soda and salt; mix until blended. Divide dough, wrap each half in plastic wrap and pat into disk. Refrigerate several hours until firm. On a floured surface roll one disc about ¼ " thick. Cut cookies. Bake on ungreased cookie sheet in a preheated oven 325 F 12-15 minutes or until barely brown. Cool.

Icing
In bowl with mixer on low, beat 2 1/2 cups powdered sugar, ¼ teaspoon cream of tartar, and 2 large egg whites until slightly thickened. Divide icing among as many bowls as colors desired; tint with food-coloring. Keep bowls covered with plastic wrap to prevent icing from drying.

Acknowledgements

I'm deeply grateful for the weekly support for Tea Time for Your Soul ministry. Sheila Wyatt designed and maintains the webpage. She has a servant's heart and is my co-worker in Christ along with Terry Heard and Elizabeth Knight. Both of these special women proof my last-minute writings with love and grace. I'm grateful to my daughter Rachel Farrow who has contributed the final mark-up for this book.

About the Author

I hope your soul has been transformed through the seasons of Advent and Christmastime. It has been an honor to walk through this season with you. I pray the transformation for your soul will be fruitful in the new year.

Dr. Deborah Newman

Deborah Newman is the author of Comfortable in Your Own Skin—Making Peace With Your Body, How to Really Love God as Your Father, Loving Your Body, Passion on Purpose, A Woman's Search for Worth, Then God Created Woman, and co-author of Beauty Secrets—Tips for Teens from the Ultimate Makeup Artist , Passages of Marriage, Love is a Choice Workbook, Day by Day Love is a Choice, and The Thin Disguise along with several self-published books on Amazon.com. Deborah enjoys writing a weekly devotion for www.teatimeforyoursoul.com (the same devotion is posted at www.soulsistertime.blogspot.com). She has contributed to numerous magazines and book projects. She has been a guest on television and radio, including *New Life Live*, and *Focus on the Family*. She has had the privilege to lead seminars and retreats across the country and internationally.

Find Dr. Newman
on Social Media

Twitter @soulsistertime

Facebook
Tea Time for Your Soul

Amazon and
Amazon Kindle

Website: teatimeforyoursoul.com

Made in the USA
Middletown, DE
29 November 2019